Combat Trauma: The Spousal Response to PTSD

Diana Rahe Taylor
& Dr. James D. Johnson

Combat Trauma: The Spousal Response to PTSD
By Diana Rahe Taylor & Dr. James D. Johnson

Library of Congress Control Number: 2015911597
ISBN 978-0-692-49250-5

FIRST PRINTING

Printed in the U.S.A. by Thomson-Shore, Dexter, MI

TABLE OF CONTENTS

Acknowledgements

Life takes many twists and turns, and such has been the case in the development of this book. I hadn't intended to write it, but when Jim Johnson suggested I do so, I thought why not. I soon found out it was hard work, but a labor of love. Most certainly I could not have done it without the women and men who made major contributions to the content of this book. One who is not mentioned in this book is Donna Goodrich, a professional writer and editor. Donna critiqued every page, every word and graciously offered her advice. Furthermore, she critiqued the book several times, some chapters over and over. I could not have done it without her encouragement and editorial expertise. Thank you Donna.

Dr. James Johnson, who co-authored this book, critiqued its content and encouraged me. He graciously allowed me to quote from his book *Combat Trauma: A Personal Look at Long-Term Consequences.* In fact, *Combat Trauma: The Spousal Response to Post Traumatic Stress Disorder* has from its genesis been intended as a companion to Jim's book. Jim's keen eye and expertise in counseling channeled my suggestions especially in the avenues of helps for those living with someone who suffers from PTSD. Jim, thank you for your trust and encouragement. And many thanks to "Saint" Barbara (Jim's wife) for putting up with the two of us.

Most assuredly, I wish to thank my "warrior," my wonderful husband, Charlie Taylor, whose patience and critical eye for detail kept me on target. His encouragement gently pushed me to complete the task even when I felt overwhelmed. I am proud of him and his service to our great country. He is the love of my life, my greatest fan, and my dearest friend. Thanks, honey! I love you!

As you read the book you will come across the work of Ron Miriello. His labor of love and the pursuit of truth is invaluable. He is a man who serves, relentlessly serves. He served as seaman in Vietnam— a River Rat—and serves now as a civilian by speaking the truth. He faithfully serves as a guard for conscientious and reliable truth about the war and the men who served. Not only did he allow me to use his carefully gleaned and meticulously stated research, but he often encouraged me to stay the course and finish the book. His wife is one of the many who shared their story. Thank you—both of you.

Another man who became an essential and prolific contributor is Dan Galde. Dan who served as a pararescueman with the Air Force shared much from his personal experience and edited the book with the eye of an experienced writer. Mary, to whom Dan had been married during his service years, also boosted my enthusiasm for the project. Dan is a true hero, a highly decorated hero. He was one of the hand-picked warriors who participated in the Son Tay Raid in North Vietnam to free POWs. I could not have done this book without him. Dan retired from the Air Force and now lives in our neighborhood. God is good! Thank you Dan and Mary.

Terry Gander whose patient and speedy responses to my emails and who shared bits and pieces of his story, also brought much joy and laughter into my solitary days before the computer screen. His wife, Donna, and her sister, Pam, were a great source of encouragement as well as material. Thank you one and all!

Another couple who went above and beyond were Terry and Barbe Balfe. They were a great source of experience which they graciously shared. Terry, a humble hero, and Barbe his faithful wife, friend, and companion intentionally and lovingly give a helping hand to other veterans in need, most especially the Vietnam veterans. They were immensely helpful and always readily available to assist me in anyway they could. Thank you!

Another who has made the full circle is Barbara Cannode and along with her, her husband Daniel. They serve and have served faithfully with the Military Order of the Purple Heart. Thank you Barbara and Dan for your service then and now.

Thank you, June Carolus for the very moving and articulate poetry which you contributed. Her husband, Jim, a Marine, served two tours in Vietnam. I will ever be grateful to the two of you—for your stories that show the pain of your heartaches and shed light to the heartaches that others have endured, the poetry that brings tears to our eyes, and warmth of your friendship—thanks.

One more – JoAnn Moore whose emails kept me glued to the computer and whose encouragement pushed me to complete the final draft. You and Guy inspired me to continue the project. Thank you for sharing from your joys and sorrows. Now that it is complete—thank you!

The book would never have come together without the men and women who contributed their stories. All have gone the extra mile. While I have not listed each by name, I will ever be grateful to all of them. I will never stop singing their praises.

You're always *One Choice*
Away from changing your life.
Mac Anderson

INTRODUCTION

Dr. James D. Johnson published two books. The first was *Combat Chaplain: A Thirty Year Vietnam Battle* (University of North Texas Press, 2001) and the second was *Combat Trauma: A Personal Look at Long-Term Consequences* (Roman and Littlefield Publishing Group, Inc., 2010). I (Diana) have read both of them.

After reading both of these books, I had the privilege of sitting and discussing their content with him. I said, "Jim, now you need to write a book for the wives and family members. People, especially other wives, who are or have been married to combat veterans need to know there is hope and help for them and their families."

Jim replied, "I hear you, but I can't write it. You're the wife of a combat vet. You write it."

"I will, but will you be the co-author?" I responded with both fear of the task that lay before me and grateful for an opportunity to honor the brave warriors who fought in Vietnam and their families who have loved them sacrificially.

"Yes," Jim replied.

So here we are—eighteen of us—fifteen wives of combat veterans who all proudly served in Vietnam and one who is a sister and another who is a sister-in-law of a warrior,. Another wife (number eighteen) is the wife of a combat veteran who served two tours in the Iraqi war. (For good reason, "Amy" wishes to remain anonymous.) Some of us are married to the men whose combat histories are told in Dr. Johnson's book *Combat Trauma*. All of us have been to hell and back with our combat veteran spouses.

Some have suffered through divorce. Some men, who are presently married, bear the cross of previous divorces, some of the women too. While divorce carries with it an element of trauma, it is not discussed within the scope of this book. Rather, we will look at ways to build archways that may open pathways to higher ground. I mention it here because the trauma of war makes the normality of family life strained at best and often devastating.

All who are or have been married or share a caring friendship with a combat veteran, hallow their service and strive to bring tranquility into their lives. It is our earnest endeavor to bring hope into the lives of other combat veterans and their families.

Within the pages of this book are the stories of husbands and wives whose lives and hearts have been ravaged by combat. At times they despaired of finding peace or connection with one another. So destructive are these unseen forces that they often obliterate reason. One may wonder if a fire-breathing dragon who leaps from the hall closet from time to time has taken up permanent residency, hanging around solely to destroy all that is good and worth living for.

If that is your story, allow us to come alongside you so that you might take the journey with us. There is hope, we know. Through trial and error, patience and fortitude, we have found a comfortable and loving companionship—not perfect, but something worth nurturing. Such is a rare and valued endeavor. So, this is a book about living with a warrior who anguishes from Post-Traumatic Stress (PTS), Post-Traumatic Stress Disorder (PTSD), and in some cases Traumatic Brain Injury (TBI). It brings together the experiences of women who have lived and suffered with men who served in Vietnam, who came home to a virulent society, insensitive Veterans Administration, and wishy-washy government.

Allow us to show you the way.

Post-Traumatic Stress Disorder: What Is It?

Post Traumatic Stress and its variants are the seen and unseen manifestations of a "disease" of the heart and soul of a man or woman sustained on the battlefield and engraved on the psyche and body. It is destructive and long-term. The effects of physical and emotional trauma may be treated, and they may heal, but they will leave scars that are forever apparent to the sufferer and their family. Post-Traumatic Stress doesn't go away, but it can be managed.

In reality, PTSD is a family disease, not unlike alcoholism and drug addiction is a family disease. By this, we mean that the symptoms of PTSD are impacted and often absorbed by the family members of a PTSD-infected veteran.

Mary Galde says, "There were several traumatic situations for Dan—both while in Vietnam and also during the course of his career in noncombat situations. Being in the rescue field, he witnessed many horrific things. On one occasion he was tasked to pick up the pieces of an American pilot who had been severed in half at the waist with a crash. When stationed in California, he had to pick up the bodies of nineteen deceased and badly burned victims of a plane crash."

When Dan was in Vietnam, he rescued downed pilots, and on one occasion, searched for underwater bodies in the Mekong River. He personally survived a helicopter crash landing in Laos. After months of training, he and several other pararescuemen participated in the Son Tay Raid, only to find once they reached the prison that the prisoners were gone. It was later he learned that they had not been executed, but had been moved to another prison camp known as the "Hanoi Hilton."

"It was devastating," says Mary. "I could tell the physical and emotional toll just by looking at him. All I knew to do was hold him and tell him everything would be okay. I knew, though, that my hugs couldn't take away what he'd been through."

Dan Galde, like thousands of others who served in Vietnam, suffers with PTSD and is presently in counseling at the Veterans Administration Center. His training kept him alive, but post-war traumatic stress has taken its toll.

In January 2003 Bob Stumpf was placed in a twenty-six day PTSD program at the Batavia Veterans Medical Center, Batavia, New York. He said, "The Batavia program helped me to understand and define what was and still is going on in my life. They taught me coping skills and made me feel safe in an environment and place that I never knew existed. That was a parachute for me and a safety net."[1]

Dr. James Johnson spent twenty years as a chaplain in the military and fifteen years as therapist/pastoral counselor before retirement. In 2005, when he was at the "height of overwhelming resurgence of feelings from Vietnam, it was his Vietnam buddy Bob Stumpf who strongly encouraged him to enter the Batavia, New York, inpatient program."[2] Jim says essentially the same thing about his PTS treatment as does Bob.

These are real stories about real people whose struggles and successes may mirror yours. Let our confessions awaken within you, not only prospects of a better future, but trust and love in your hearts and homes as it has done in ours.

For the sake of clarity, the bulk of this book is written in the first person of *Diana*.

THE CO-AUTHORS

As mentioned above, Dr. James D. Johnson has authored two books that have touched a nerve in almost every combat veteran who has read them. He holds a masters degree in counseling and a doctorate in marriage and family counseling. After a twenty-year career with the Army as chaplain, he served fifteen years with the staff of a large church in Fayetteville, North Carolina as therapist/pastoral counselor. He served as a combat chaplain with the 3/60th Infantry Battalion, 9th Infantry Division during the Vietnam War (1967-1968), experiencing almost constant combat conditions in the Delta region of South Vietnam. He chose to go out with his infantrymen on every combat operation, although never carrying a weapon. He was awarded three Bronze Medals and the Air Medal. He and his wife, Barbara, presently live in Fayetteville, where they enjoy several grandchildren as well as their four adult children.

I, Diana Rahe Taylor, have authored several magazine and newspaper articles, but my claim to fame is my husband, Charlie, who served as an infantry officer with the Bandido Charlie (C Company 5/60th Mechanized Infantry Battalion) in South Vietnam from June 1967 through June 1968. Charlie and Jim were together in numerous battles with the enemy. He is a much decorated hero, having received the Combat Infantryman's Badge, two Bronze Stars for Valor, two Purple Hearts, the Air Medal, the Army Commendation Medal, and the RVN Gallantry Cross Unit Citation. His story can be read in Dr. Johnson's latest book *Combat Trauma: A Personal Look at Long-Term Consequences.*

After leaving the Army, we moved back to our hometown of Prescott, Arizona. Nineteen years ago, we settled into the small nearby country community of Skull Valley, Arizona. Both of us are Certified Financial Planners. I was involved in financial and retirement counseling and teaching until I retired for health reasons, with the encouragement of my beloved husband, I followed my dream of writing. We have two adult sons, a lovely daughter-in-law, and two beautiful grandchildren.

Both Jim and I have had significant life-threatening health issues in the past. In 1995 I was diagnosed with stage 3 non-Hodgkin's lymphoma. At one point of my fight to live, I was in a coma for ten days and on oxygen. By the grace of God, I am alive and well today. Jim has had cardiac bypass surgery, lost a kidney due to cancer, has a serious blood disorder which has threatened his life several times and more recently had a pituitary tumor removed from his brain.

We both feel very strongly that God has not taken us yet because He is not through with us. So, here we are…

WE EIGHTEEN—WHO WE ARE

Barbara Balfe: Holland Patent, New York. Barbara married Terry Balfe after he returned from Vietnam where he served with B Company, 3 Battalion 60 Infantry. While Terry worked his way up to being a postmaster, Barbara was lucky enough to be a stay-at-home mom. Barbara admits to being a tad prejudiced, but she thinks keeping him around was well worth the trials and tribulations. What's their secret—"keeping in touch with one another's heartstrings." She is ever so thankful that Terry has finally come to terms with earning two Purple Hearts and the Silver Star.

Barbara Bedell: Rio Vista, California. Barbara married William Metzler "Metz" in 1986 many years after he had returned from the war. He served as RTO with B Company of the 5th Battalion, 60th Infantry. And while he fought in many battles, nothing surpasses his experience at Fire Base Jaeger, February 25[3]. Metz has been blessed with an incredible gift for finding humor in the most outrageous circumstances. Barbara and Metz were dental hygienists for thirty-plus years. They worked together in the same office. Now that they are retired, Barbara spends her time doing exactly as she pleases—yoga, bicycling, reading, meditating, playing cards and computer games, going for walks and making day trips around the delta. Metz jokes that he is once again in the Delta (Vietnam).

Barbara Cannode: Waterville, Ohio. Barbara and Daniel were married two weeks before Daniel left for Vietnam. He served with the United States Coast Guard Squadron One, Div. 13, Cat Lo, RVN. Barbara has served as the national president for the Ladies Auxiliary Military Order of the Purple Heart. She has served in positions of department resident State of Ohio, department Ohio junior and senior ice, chaplain and region II president over eleven states. In September 2010 four people were asked to speak to a group of psychologist and counselors at the VA Hospital in Ann Arbor, Michigan and Barbara had the privilege of being one of those four. She was recently interviewed by Ursula Buzzacca, an undergraduate student at Walsh Catholic University in North Canton, Ohio. The interview will be stored in the Library of Congress Veterans' Oral History Project and, in the future, with the Ohio Historical Society's Memory Project.

June Carolus: Greeley, Colorado, whose husband, Jim, served two tours in Vietnam. His first tour from May 1965 to June 1966 was with Alpha Company, 1st Platoon 9th Marines—known as the "Walking Dead." The second tour, January 1968 to March 1969, was with HMMS14 where he served as staff sergeant. Jim Carolus retired from the Marines as a first sergeant in 1997. June is a poet and a promising author of children's literature. Her poetry speaks to the soul. Three poems are included in this book.

Sally C.: Anonymous

Mary Galde: Milpitas, CA. Dan Galde served with the USAF pararescue organization throughout South East Asia from 1963-1970, three years in Vietnam. Besides rescuing downed pilots and reclaiming body parts, he was chosen for participation in the Son Tay Raid into North Vietnam with the intent of rescuing American POWs. His Air Force career spanned twenty-one years in various places all over the world, during which he received a Silver Star, Distinguished Flying Cross, Bronze Star, five Air Medals and many other awards and decorations. He retired in 1983 as a senior master sergeant. Mary and Dan have been divorced for many years, but maintain contact with each other and their three sons. Mary works for JDSU as an administrative assistant, but hopes to retire within the year.

Donna Gander: Evansville, Indiana. Donna and Terry Gander[4] married on December 3, 2006. Terry served as a rifleman with B Company, 3rd Battalion, 60th Infantry. When Terry married Donna, he married into a family of saints. Donna is a devoted, loving wife, and her siblings are some of Terry's greatest supporters, especially Pam, Donna's sister. Donna's brother, Kip Husk, adopted Terry as his "hero" for the Ft. Branch 9/11 Event. The deserved veneration this family holds for Terry and his service is nothing short of total inspiration.

Barbara Johnson: Fayetteville, North Carolina. When Jim deployed for Vietnam, he left behind beautiful Barbara and two children. Jim served as chaplain for the 3/60 Infantry Battalion, one of the few chaplains to serve beside the fighting men in the field. Barbara faithfully kept the home fires burning and the letters and tapes flowing back and forth to Vietnam. She is a homemaker with all the Southern pizzazz you can imagine. For years she worked as a dental hygienist. She is now retired—from the dental business, not from Jim. Jim has had a number of major health issues, and right beside him is Barbara—dedicated and loving as an angel.

Debbie Miriello: Sanford, North Carolina. Debbie and Ron met in college and married in 1973 after his service. Ron served as a U.S. Navy "River Rat" with the River Assault Division 91 and 92. He was a 50 Caliber machine gunner on an ATC (Armored Troop Carriers) and on an ASPB (Assault Support Patrol Boat). After Vietnam he was employed for thirty years in higher education in various positions of administration. Since retirement, he has taken on a new mission— *Vietnam: The Way it Was—a Combat Veteran's Perspective.* As a speaker, Ron endeavors "to inform, educate, and enlighten audiences on the most misrepresented, misunderstood, and forgotten war of modern time." Debbie retired from teaching and tutoring in 2013. She is a supportive wife and a devoted mother to their children Diana and Mark. Check out Ron's website at www.vietnamriverrat.com.

JoAnn Moore: formerly of Saugatuck, Michigan, but now live year round in Phoenix, Arizona. She married Guy P. Moore in 1975—a significant time lapse after the Vietnam War. Guy P.[5] served as a rifleman and radio operator in B Company, 3rd Battalion, 60th Infantry, burying himself by working twelve- to fourteen-hour days and most often seven days a week. Guy was awarded the Purple Heart. JoAnn has been Guy P.'s rock , standing by him through the "buried" times and the "flare ups.". She loves to knit and tend her Mary Kay business.

Lynne Moseman: Athens, Georgia. Lynne and Roy met while in their early teens and married within a few years of his return from Vietnam. They have been married for over forty years. Roy[6] served as a rifleman, radio operator, squad leader, and platoon sergeant with C Company of the 4th Battalion, 47th Infantry. He owned Classic Electrical Contracting prior to retirement. Lynne said, "Roy and I love each other and nothing is going to change that aspect of our marriage, not even Roy's battle with PTSD." Lynne retired after fourteen years of working at University Testing Services, serving as a computer based test administrator. Prior to working for the University of Georgia, she—along with a business partner—owned a small wholesale business. They have one son who is career military.

Janett McBroom Olivares: Janett's father, Staff Sgt. George E. Fowler, was a photographer and waist gunner in the 15th Air Force on B-24 bombers over Ploesti. On his 24th mission, 6 May 1944, he was shot down over Romania, wounded and became a prisoner of war. He remained a POW until 31 August, 1944. He was awarded a Purple Heart Medal, Soldier's Medal, Air Medal, and Good Conduct Medal. Janett's brother, Geoffrey E. Fowler, served in Vietnam with the 1st Aviation Brigade, Black Cats as a Crew Chief on a Chinook. He received a Purple Heart and a Bronze Star. After being wounded and a lengthy recovery, he became a commercial pilot. He flew as a corporate pilot for many years. He died in 2002 at age 50 after several years of failed treatments for alcoholism. Janett had been a successful Realtor in Prescott, AZ for almost 20 years and now lives in Southern

California. She is semi-retired with a new home-based career that allows her to travel and spend time with her children, grandchildren and her 95 year old mom, Patricia Fowler.

Pam Rogers: Troutman, North Carolina. Pam is an independent consultant, project manager, and corporate advocate in the healthcare industry, currently on assignment at the University of Southern California Norris Cancer and Keck Hospitals, in Los Angeles, California. She is sister to Donna Gander and confidante to Terry Gander. Pam is married to Garry, and they travel extensively in the NASCAR circuit. She is also a cheerleader to Garry who, in his spare time, is a professional angler in the Bassmaster Southern Opens and other tournament venues throughout the year. She has one son, Chad, who lives in Evansville, Indiana, with his wife of ten years, Shaunda. Pam is extremely blessed to be a "Nana" to their two beautiful sons, Hunter (7) and Marshall (1), and looks forward to her true "golden retirement years" when she will be able to spend more time with her extensive family and network of friends.

Marianne: Marianne and Bill have celebrated almost fifty years of marriage. Bill served from 1966-1968 in Vietnam with the 1st Brigade 101 Airborne, A Troop, 2/17 Cavalry. His MOS was a "scout". The 1st Brigade was known as the Nomads of Vietnam because they never stayed in one place very long. Marianne is an accomplished author with a number of books published. Her book entitled *Raven's Light~A Tale of Alaska's White Raven*, Publication Consultants, 2008 an allegory about PTSD is well worth the read. She is a registered nurse and has served in that capacity for forty-seven years.

Ella Schoenian: Glendale, West Virginia. Married to Dave (Harry) Schoenian. Dave served as a rifleman, squad leader, and platoon sergeant with the C/4/47th Infantry, then worked with the power company prior to having to retire. Ella and Dave raised three children. Dave would say that Ella carried the heavy load by herself many times. Along the way, she also accumulated three bachelor degrees. Dave said, "I've always said being the wife of a combat veteran is the toughest job there is. Being married to a combat veteran for 41 years is quite an accomplishment, carrying with it many scars." They persevered. Dave would tell you he's the lucky one. Both suffer from health issues, but they work at life together and are especially fond of being with their grandkids. Dave said, "God gave me a second chance, and God gave me Ella to guide us through life's journey."

Diana Taylor: Skull Valley, Arizona. Diana and Charlie were married three years when Charlie[7] left for Vietnam. He served with C Company (the Bandidos) 5/60 Infantry Battalion. Diana retired from her financial planning business nineteen years ago and has since followed a long-time dream of writing.

Susan Tuzcu: Delray Beach, Florida. Susan and Erol met and married many years after Erol's service in Vietnam. Erol[8] grew up in Turkey, immigrated at age eighteen, and was barely able to speak English when he was inducted into the Army. He served with A Company, 3/60 Infantry Battalion. He owns and operates U.S. Truss, Inc., and Susan is part owner of Diamond Antique Oriental Rugs.

But eagerly desire the greater gifts—love.
And now I will show you the most excellent way.
1 Corinthians 12:31 (Life Application Bible)

CHAPTER 1
The Journey Begins

The United States military is extremely well prepared for service during war or peace on our shores or abroad. Basic and advanced training prepares our military physically and psychologically. Their bodies and skills are honed to meet life and death situations. Like the parachute to the paratrooper, their training is vital to the continuation of life.

The intense training must become ingrained in the brain and the muscles, and it must manifest itself in the actions of the trainee under life-threatening situations. They learn to perform automatically and with preciseness when the need arises. Second to none, is the strong camaraderie between those in the warriors' platoon. "I have your back" may be the very thing that saves the life of the individual warrior and his buddy by his side. The paratrooper depends on the efficiency and accuracy of everyone and everything that operates between him, the jump, and the landing. The grunt on the battlefield depends on his weapon and everyone who stands between him and the success of the mission.

Our warrior-husbands were well trained. Their weapons and comrades served them well, and yet many of them have been prey to the trauma of battle. War was and is a relentless, insatiable consumer of men's hearts and souls. Remember, we may remove the man physically from the war zone, but we cannot take the warrior out of the man. And in most cases, we cannot erase their war experiences from their memories.

One does not walk away from combat without being seriously injured physically and/or emotionally. These injuries may have lifelong residual effects. The goal is to apply and modify these life-engrained activities so as to show respect and love for the "other" person, whether they are a wife, a child, or a friend. Likewise the warrior who fulfills his or her duty to our country has the right to be honored and respected by our nation's citizenry.

~ * ~ * ~ * ~

In April 1967 Charlie received his deployment orders for Vietnam. As an infantry officer he was assured a frontline battle assignment. And only God would know the full extent of Charlie's experience and the risk to life and limb he would encounter. Only God could know the post-traumatic stress that would create havoc in our home years after the war was over.

I shed many tears that first night after he received his orders, but by morning my resiliency surfaced. I packed my parachute with faith in God, donned my jumpsuit, and headed for the plane. God willing we would be together in the future. The war might separate us, but it would not crush us.

God had, as surely as I breathe, given me the assurance that Charlie would be returning home at the end of his year of service to our country in the hostile battlegrounds of Vietnam. When doubts assailed during our separation, God's voice rang clear and loud. He was in control; I need only trust Him. And so I did. What I didn't know, nor did I suspect, was who Charlie would become after his encounter with this deadly force we call war.

Charlie left for Southeast Asia in June 1967, six weeks before our third wedding anniversary and a few weeks before his twenty-fifth birthday. He sent me a picture of himself sitting to the side of his APC (armored personnel carrier) celebrating with a smile on his face and dining in high style, eating one of those delicious pound cakes—a staple in the C-rations. I later sent a pecan pie that I'd carefully packed in popcorn. (I've been told it arrived whole and was greatly appreciated by Charlie and his platoon.)

As you would expect, my recollections of the war differs greatly from that of Charlie's. For Charlie, now forty-plus years after his return from the battlefields, the horrors of war are vivid and corrosive. Like a stuck computer program that refuses to move to the next screen, his memories haunt him. Yet when I hear or read the stories of other wives of combat veterans, I realize I'm one of the lucky ones. Charlie returned to a family who loved him. They were not in any way curious about his experience in Vietnam, but they received him home with open arms. He had, after all, performed his duty to his country. The same can be said of his church family and the community. There were no parades, but neither were there any obnoxious bystanders spouting obscenities and gross, misguided—if not outright—lies. This is what I did observe:

When Charlie returned from Vietnam, he wrapped his hellish memories up in a tight bundle and stashed it in the recesses of his mind. Only occasionally did he speak of his experiences or behave in a manner foreign to him before his year at war, but I was not deceived. Naive, yes, but not blind. Embedded in his psyche never to be forgotten were unspeakable, despicable menacing memories. Over the years their impact has lessened, but they have never been replaced. I'm not sure they should be. He acted bravely and with honor. War is hell anyway you cut it.

When our warriors came home from Vietnam, most wives and girlfriends sailed to their sides with strong winds of hope for a bright future. The war was behind us—or so we thought. However, time and intimacy soon stripped away our blindness and our high expectations. Common to many of us was an incredible level of ignorance, in spite of the fact that the daily news carried graphic reports of the war. Many of us didn't know much about Vietnam, its history or its battlefield. Furthermore, once our warriors returned home we lost interest in the war—at least at first, and then the paper walls began to tear. That came for some sooner than for others.

When Charlie left for Vietnam, I headed back to college. In the year I was there only one person asked me about his welfare. And strangely the church I attended never mentioned the war. It is very possible they prayed for them, but I do not remember them doing so. When he returned, we drove off to our next duty assignment. He trained troops and I became a little homemaker. All seemed well…well, for a while all seemed well.

Barbe Balfe was fifteen years old when she first met Terry. She thought he was a man of the world. At the age of eighteen he left for Vietnam. Unlike most teens Barbe was extremely aware of the Vietnam War since she had a cousin there. Several fellow employees with whom she worked with at a restaurant went into the military and were eventually sent to Vietnam. One of them was beheaded when he drove through a wired booby trap. The nightly news and body counts were definitely on her radar.

Barbe said, "I was a kid, just sixteen years old when Terry and I started to date. I was naïve about the war. I did tell Terry that I was glad I was born a girl and didn't have to fight in one. I also thanked him for keeping me safe. And I do the same today for those brave young men and women who are serving in the armed forces so I can live this wonderful life in the U.S.

"After we started dating, Terry would tell me of some of his experiences. He would say he was scared shitless and kinda laugh about it," Barbe said. "It wasn't until thirty-five years or so later that his true emotions began to come out. I always feel overwhelmingly sad when Terry talks of the 'crap' he went through. I am at a loss of what to say or how to act to make him feel better and yet, at the same time, I know there's not much I can say."

It is a far reach from a school dance to an eighteen-year-old infantryman, shot four times and lying all night within a yard or two of the enemy who but by the grace of God would have either killed him or captured him. Yet, Barbe and Terry have been able to rectify the differences of time, place, and experiences to make a good life for themselves and their children.

On the other hand, many teens worried about their social activities and their attire, but had little interest in the war—other than avoiding the draft. And why should they? Don't we usually shield children from the horrors of war?

June Carolus didn't know her husband Jim when he served in Vietnam. They met and married later. He served two tours and like any effective and disciplined Marine sergeant, he felt responsible for the lives of the men who served under him. He blames himself because he lived and many of them died. It wasn't until he and June were married that he talked about Vietnam. Even now his story comes in bits and pieces.

Lynne Moseman says, "Roy never talked about any of the unpleasant aspects of being a nineteen-year-old soldier in a major combat zone. However, he would share some funny stories about the guys he served with and different things they did to entertain themselves in the field. These men were really just boys and when they had a chance to act like kids, they usually did."

Like many men, Roy suffers from nightmares and has for the entire forty years that he and Lynne have been married. "I knew he never slept well," Lynne says. "But we were fifteen years into our marriage before he shared his nightmare with me. He constantly dreams that he is back in Vietnam and can't leave the country because his paperwork isn't in order."

When speaking with Dan Galde about parachuting, he commented on the uncertainty of the landing. "Landing zones are the only uncontrollable element in parachuting," he said. "All other components are micromanaged by highly trained and experienced parachutists."

I wish the same could be said about the combat veteran. Returning after their tour in Vietnam, they jumped without a fully functioning parachute into a society that failed them miserably.

Barbara Cannode, whose husband served in Vietnam with the Coast Guard, says, "My emotions from combat trauma…hurt, sadness. Anger with our government for taking this wonderful young man I married and sending home to me someone I did not know. Anger over the loss of our tender relationship. Confusion as to what to do and how to think. Yes, I am DAMN mad."

Daniel Cannode served with the U.S. Coast Guard Squadron One, Div. 13, Cat Lo, RVN. His job, and that of his comrades, was to search all sampan traffic in multiple river and canal locations. His duties took him below the decks of the sampans, out of view of the crew and armed with nothing but a K-Bar and a .45. They performed this duty day in and day out, encountering night ambushes and providing fire support for army units. Horrendous encounters continue to haunt his thoughts and dreams.

Erol Tuzcu refused to talk about his experience in Vietnam from the time he and Susan met in December 1978 until after he returned from a Mobile Riverine Reunion in 1999. When quizzed he would say, "We did terrible things over there." End of conversation.

In 1999 Erol attended the reunion at the behest of his former commanding officer, Milton Keene. He had been leery and nervous about going and did not want Susan to accompany him.

"That reunion helped him immensely," Susan said. "His attitude changed when he got back. In 2001, I went with him to the next reunion and on the way, as he was driving, I read to him from Jim Johnson's first book *Combat Chaplain: A Thirty-Year Vietnam Battle*. Erol was amazed and kept saying to me, 'That's exactly what we went through!'"

With awe in her voice, Susan said, "Reading that book was my first inkling of what happened to Erol and all of his comrades in arms over there. I think every person who knows a Vietnam vet needs to read it!"

Remember this book you're now reading is a follow-up to Dr. Johnson's second book, *Combat Trauma: A Personal Look at Long-Term Consequences,* a book that illuminates the ghoulishness that combat perpetrates upon the hearts and psyche of brave, young men, some on the ragged edges of their teen years. They were boys who became men after their first firefight, and weathered and worn warriors after mere days and numerous combat encounters.

In looking back to that evening when Charlie stepped off the plane in Phoenix, I realize my thoughts were pure and my expectations were simple. I anticipated a bright and beautiful stream of tomorrows. The prospects of an unmarred future now seems incredibly immature and naïve. Yet I was not unlike most wives.

When our warriors came home, we thought the battlefields were behind us. Little did I know the war would haunt our warriors night and day. Nothing was sacred. They were like targets on a shooting range, waiting for the next shot to tear away their hearts and souls.

For a warrior to even try to forget wartime trauma—whether it be in Vietnam, Iraq, Afghanistan, or the phantom terrorist, the horror and the blood and guts so innate to war—is like pretending he was never born or that he didn't attend school. Such is not reality, and it is not going to change over time. Furthermore, how the warrior deals with the end results is uniquely personal and permanent. How we, the spouses of combat veterans, respond is an issue to be considered with deep introspection. To pretend it didn't affect our children and us is laughable. Counseling with someone familiar with post-traumatic stress is advisable.

Allow me to emphasize that as we move through this book, our response to our warriors will be one of validation, honor, and respect. Our warriors are men of integrity. Their experiences are worth remembering, but with caution. Within the rehash lies dangerous and destructive lies as well as truth. How and what the warrior remembers, his reaction to those memories—the good and the bad—and where he places the blame should be considered with an eye for healing.

The same can be said to us, the spouses and loving companions of these brave men. We have a powerful influence on our long-term relationship with our warrior-husbands. But we must beware of "compassion fatigue." Setting healthy boundaries for ourselves and for our warriors is essential. (More on that later.)

When I look back over my own response to Charlie's return, I see a starry-eyed young wife without a clue about his experiences. I couldn't ask reasonably intelligent questions, so I didn't ask anything. Like many warriors, he didn't talk about his traumatic experience. He stuffed it. And I, in my naiveté, wanted nothing less than the typical American "Ozzie and Harriet" marriage and family life. For the most part, Charlie's quiet demeanor allowed me to live unscathed within our charmed marriage. For some of you, it was like a roadside bomb exploding, sending shrapnel far and near injuring and often killing your hopes and dreams. In most case, you didn't see it coming, and when it came, you didn't know what to do about it.

Knowing society and government wouldn't listen to the cries of emotionally wounded veterans, we too learned to stuff our pain. No one believed us. No one—and I mean no one—wanted to know our stories. No one wanted to hear about our emotions and frustrations. When all hell broke loose in the sanctuary of our homes, we had no-where to go and no one to turn to. To reveal our stories and our innermost fears was to solicit criticism. To speak openly about the trauma in our homes was to invite the perception of a character in Looney Tunes. Speaking out was little more than a petition for more trouble. It wasn't worth it. And the truth is, no one had answers.

So the years ticked by, one by one. The Vietnam veteran went into a holding pattern, much like an airliner circling the landing strip waiting for the air controller to give permission to land. For many the fuel ran out. The plane crashed taking the passengers with it. For some it took years, but the day came when good men who had worked hard, raised families, and simply made life work, fell apart. Then and only then did the government and the Veterans Administration recognize the crisis, calling it post- traumatic stress (PTS) or post-traumatic stress disorder (PTSD). Many wives suffer from secondary PTSD.

Some of the greatest men I know are those veterans who have suffered wounds of the heart, the soul, and the spirit. These are warriors whose core values are admirable and honorable, yet evil demanded a great price from them. It would seem the greater their goodness, the deeper their wounds. War raped the minds and hearts of these kind and gentle-spirited men, men with integrity and courage, men who stood the course regardless of the danger. With time, encouragement, and support from spouses, family members, and professional counselors I believe these men will find an inner balance that will build and rebuild their resolve for straighter, stronger backbones. And we, their wives (even women who have divorced the warrior), may harvest great benefits from standing by these heroes as together we weather the storms of their turmoil and struggle to find healing.

If you are a combat veteran or you are living with a combat veteran, you've probably been to hell and back several times over. In fact, you may feel your family room is adjacent to hell's front door. You may feel that a command-detonated bomb explodes periodically and shrapnel decimates your home...and your heart. May you glean hope and inspiration from our experiences.

Suppose I speak in the languages of
human beings and of angels.
If I don't have love, I am only a
loud gong or a noise cymbal.
1 Corinthians 13:1

CHAPTER 2
Myths—Lies

"When I came home from Vietnam, I was made to feel like an outcast," said Guy P. Moore.

"Leading men in combat in Vietnam was the most defining experience of my life, but within a few weeks of returning home, I discovered no one cared," said Charlie Taylor.

Bundled into these rejections were a pack of lies and myths about the war. Unfortunately, it was the men and women who served in horrifying life-and-death situations who shouldered the brunt of a society's vehemence. Why?

Vietnam—who wrote the surreal script? Who pulled the ensnarled strings? Military Assistance Command Vietnam (MACV)? General Westmoreland? Certainly not the American GI. One has only to read the history books to know the government and the childish counterculture of society jerked the chains as the GI dodged death and destruction. It was Congress and the president who played hot and cold, cat and mouse using the GI as political bait in a mismanaged war. Society labeled the GI an unworthy low-crawling creature. Our government wanted to oust Communism from potential world domination. The hippies and other antiwar groups claimed to hate war, but in reality their main purpose seemed to be steering away from being drafted into the military. It was the American GIs, honoring their call to duty, who dangled on the end of the rope and who in the end paid the piper. The tally of the times? Lies! Myths! Chaos!

The Vietnam veteran, with guts and little glory, fought a heinous war under miserable physical and emotional conditions, then came home to a malevolent society, a wishy-washy government, and an unsympathetic Veterans Administration. The combat veteran, often mere hours from leaving the fields of war, found himself thrust into an incomprehensible battle for dignity and respect on his home turf, unwelcomed—an instantaneous new reality. When Guy Moore came home he landed in California. Protestors threw water balloons at him. He later found out they had urine in them.

Years later, it became fashionable and rewarding to have been a Vietnam War Vet. The wannabes—the "powder puffs"—came out of their cosmetic cases and powdered their filthy lies. No one exposes and documents the truth about the wannabes better than G.B. Burkett and Glenna Whitley in their book entitled *Stolen Valor.*[9]

Dr. James Johnson in his book *Combat Trauma* says this: "For anyone to tell a lie about anything else in their lives is none of our business. But to steal the valor of our fallen brothers is a direct insult to our past. If we had our way, to do so would be a criminal offense punishable by prison. Words cannot express how livid it makes us to even hear about any of those fakes and make-believers!"[10]

Roy Moseman says: "It seems popular today to be a combat veteran fake, and they are coming out of the woodwork. I can't stand a combat wannabe, pretender, or a liar about the Vietnam experience. They are doing an injustice to the brave men and women who fought for this country while many of them stayed home and had a good time."[11]

Wannabes reaped benefits from the unsuspecting citizenry in some cases via the national network television. They cast a sort of voodoo spell on the truth. The wannabes dressed the part, said all the right things, and soon ingratiated themselves into the hearts of an unsuspecting, guilt ridden society who now struggled to defend their low esteem of the true Vietnam veteran.

Recently the Supreme Court shot down the Stolen Valor law. When the law originated, it was meant to be used as a "needed tool to protect the integrity of military medals."[12]

The lies, myths, and legal manipulation tempt me to fly into a tornado of expletives.

Without question, something is wrong with this picture. It victimized those duty-bound by oath to defend this country at the request of Congress and the president. A systemic poison infected all of society, including the families of those who served in the military. Shame! Shame! Shame!

Because the lies, myths, and wannabes stamped the Vietnam War as unjust and unlawful, our warriors found it advantageous to stuff their experiences inside. While such behavior saved them from the venomous bite of society, it proved to be hazardous to the warriors' emotional and physical well-being. Naturally, this impacted loved ones as well. Furthermore, their withdrawal unwittingly fueled further lies and myths. It wasn't until the Veterans Administration took seriously the dangers of post-traumatic stress disorder, and now, traumatic-brain injury and secondary traumatic stress, that the veterans' standing in society took a turn for the better.

Truth—Sound Bites from the Veterans

For decades our warriors suppressed their trauma because no one took them seriously or believed them. The thundering of lies and myths darkened the truth until most veterans gave up trying to be heard. Furthermore, some veterans couldn't comprehend what was happening to themselves. They couldn't put a name to it. Some felt totally alone, as if they were some one-of-a-kind oddity.

When Charlie Taylor came home from Vietnam, his community, his church, and his family welcomed him immediately, but within a few weeks, everyone had heard all they wanted to know about that war ten thousand miles away. Left unsaid, but always hanging unspoken was, "That was then; this is now; get over it."

Within a few months of returning Stateside, most combat veterans ceased to speak of their experiences. Why? No one cared about the day-to-day traumatic memories of our warriors' wartime experiences. A day at the office or a day on the golf course took precedence over the warriors' reality. Picnics and pool parties and other pleasantries were more palatable and entertaining.

No one understood me," said Roy Moseman. "Friends and family didn't know what was inside me. I didn't know how to explain it to them. Then, after a while, I didn't want to."[13]

Lynne Moseman, wife of Roy, said, "No matter how hard I try I'll never understand what Roy went through when he was in Vietnam. It's a helpless feeling because you can't change the past or make it disappear. Roy would tell me how he felt, then withdraw. For the most part, he shut me out of that part of his life."

"Roy and I have gone through a rough patch the last four or five months," Lynne said recently. "Roy's depression and anxiety had gotten worse. Fortunately, with changes to his medication the past month has been so much better. He's getting back to being himself again."

"Guy P. Moore's life of post-Vietnam rebellion began immediately, as he learned that American society was treating him like an outcast," Dr. Johnson writes. "He quickly turned into a confused, hurt, and often violent young man whom people did not want to be around. Guy actually got into a fight at a bar within hours after arriving in California from Vietnam and spent the night in jail. This was the first of numerous fights in the future that caused much difficulty for a very troubled young veteran. He had been in 'combat mode' for months and remained in that mode for years."[14]

JoAnn Moore, Guy's wife, says, "Even today he is always on watch, not so much for attacks but for people trying to cheat him. He doesn't trust anyone."

Barbara Johnson, wife of Dr. Johnson, says, "Jim learned very soon after coming home that people didn't really want to hear how it was in Vietnam. They would ask and immediately change the subject. So, he began to write. After all, if you are writing, only you can change the subject."

"For several months after returning from Vietnam, Jim did not talk about his experiences," Barbara said, "but he wrote pages and pages. He filled numerous legal pads with notes and stories. However, I was not allowed to see what he was writing. If I asked he would say something like 'I'll let you see it but not now.' I never pushed the matter. I knew it was very private, whatever it was.

"He now says he meant to be inclusive of me by showing me what he was writing, but it took three decades for that to happen."

We are forty-plus years out from the Vietnam War and still our warriors suffer. I can't help but wonder how much better off our men would have been had the Nation been more sensitive to the physiological and psychological needs when they returned. All of us— warriors, wives, and children—would have valued from intervention, whether through counseling or medication. While we cannot reclaim the past, we can learn from it. As for the veteran and family members, it is *not* too late to get assistance. Seek help now!

Truth—Sound Bites from History

It has been said that if we do not learn from history, we are doomed to repeat it. What I have found is that after forty-some years since the Vietnam War came to a close, most people only have a peripheral understanding of what really happened. I wonder, as we anticipate the close of current and future wars, if our ignorance is a window for repeating lies and myths to the detriment of our warriors. Such might be the case.

Let us look at the components and the proponents of these lies and myths. Let us examine the effect on the GI and the family members. And then let us ask ourselves what can be done to rectify the problems that plague the lives of our combat warriors and find ways to prevent them from being repeated.

Myths and Truths—A Closer Look

- Vietnam was a conflict, a minor insurgency, not a war.
- America lost the war in Vietnam.
- Vietnam vets were largely uneducated draftees.
- Vietnam vets failed to reintegrate into work and society.
- Vietnam vets are homeless, potheads who are prone to suicide.

Ron Miriello served with the U.S. Navy as a 50 caliber machine gunner on the Mobile Riverine Forces in 1968-1969. For thirty years he was employed at Fayetteville Technical Community College and Central Carolina Community College in North Carolina. He served in several capacities including vice president for educational and student service, dean of students, associate dean of students, director of admissions, director of veteran's services, veterans counselor, and adult high school and GED counselor. He is now retired and has dedicated his life to "educating and enlightening audiences on the most misrepresented, misunderstood, and forgotten war of modern time."[15]

Ron has graciously allowed me to quote from his PowerPoint presentation that meticulously documents facts about the Vietnam War and the veterans who served. The above myth/truth-statements are an extrapolation of his work and information gleaned from History.com.[16]

Perhaps we can better understand the combat veteran if we reenact the drama he faced upon his return home. These miserable, flaming myths ignited vicious hatred within society toward our heroes. Is it any wonder why our warriors suffer emotionally? While we, as spouses, may have varying degrees of knowledge and comprehension of this history, I believe a review may give us greater perspective on the issues facing the warrior when he returned to his homeland.

MYTH—pure and simple.

- Vietnam was a conflict, a minor insurgency, not a war.

Fact—Quoting from Ron Miriello's presentation: "A *conflict* is defined as a clash; to meet in opposition; to be at odds with; to differ; a prolonged struggle; strong disagreement; incompatible. *War* is defined as open armed fighting."

What was Vietnam—a war or a conflict? When my husband (Charlie Taylor) was in Vietnam, serving with the 5/60th Mechanized Infantry in the Mekong Delta and with the Mobile Riverine Force, he sent reel-to-reel tapes home. While it was a joy to hear his voice, I was also alarmed by the sounds of weapons firing in the background—incoming and outgoing shelling. This was war, not a PlayStation® clash.

Fact—statistics tell us that out of the 365 days our combat troops served in country, they saw 240 days of combat. Of the 2.59 million who served, 58,169 were killed and 304,000 were wounded. One out of every 10 Americans who served in Vietnam was a casualty.[17]

My (Diana) husband, Charlie Taylor, was wounded twice—has two Purple Hearts and two Bronze Stars for Valor. Believe me, it was not a 'conflict'—it was WAR.

"We fought in a real war, not some minor insurgency, conflict, guerilla war, limited war, police action or any name Washington came up with for the benefit of the public," Richard Sinsigalli says. "It was kill or be killed. It was a matter of survival—365 days of survival. Fifty-eight thousand two hundred thirty-five Americans were killed." (Sinsigalli is a former chief warrant officer and Army veteran who served in the Korean and Vietnam Wars. He is also the author of *Chopper Pilot: Not All of Us Were Heroes*).[18]

MYTH—

- America lost the war in Vietnam.

Fact— "No! No! No! We were not allowed to win the war!"[19]

"The U.S. did not lose the war in Vietnam, the South Vietnamese did. The fall of Saigon happened April 30, 1975, two years AFTER the American military left Vietnam. The last American troops departed Vietnam March 29, 1973. The peace settlement had been signed in Paris on January 27, 1973."[20]

"In January 1973, the Nixon administration negotiated a truce between Hanoi and Saigon, known as the Paris Peace Accords." The U.S. promised to furnish South Vietnam with aid, but reneged on that promise leaving the South Vietnamese vulnerable to the unrelenting Communist oppression.[21]

MYTH—

- Vietnam vets were largely uneducated draftees.
- Vietnam vets failed to reintegrate into work and society.

Fact – Vietnam vets were the best-educated forces our nation had ever sent into combat. Two-thirds of the men serving in Vietnam were not draftees, but volunteers—they had chosen to serve. Eighty-five percent of Vietnam Veterans made successful transitions to civilian life. It has been said that Vietnam Veterans' personal income exceeds that of our non-veteran age group by more than 18 percent."[22]

MYTH—

- Vietnam Vets are homeless, drug addicts who are prone to suicide.

Fact—"There is no difference in drug usage between Vietnam veterans and non veterans of the same age group. (a Veterans Administration study)."[23]

The above "myths" are just that—"myths." Not all Vietnam veterans commit or attempt to commit suicide. The numbers are significant and should be taken seriously. However, regardless of the percentages, even one suicide is one too many, just as one homeless veteran is one too many. No matter what the statistical conclusion, suicide, suicidal attempts, and homelessness are heartbreakers and a dark and grievous reality. Where lies the blame for such events? With the veteran? With society? With the government?

The greatest damage created by the war was the carnage of mankind's hearts, souls, and spirits. For the Vietnam veteran the horrors of war have been an everlasting flame burning within their psyche to this day. Society poured oil on that fire. And today? What will we remember? What will we have learned? Will what we have gleaned from the Vietnam theater help the next generation of combat veterans cope with their wartime experiences?

Sound Bites of the '60s and '70s

Demonstrations against the Vietnam War began in May 1964 when twelve young men in New York publically burned their draft cards. In December of 1964 six hundred protested in San Francisco. The number of protestors grew and splintered into factions, but all with the same opinion—the war was illegal and morally wrong and the draft threatened lower and middle-class registrants. Still, in early 1966 the Gallup poll showed that 59 percent of the American citizens believed that sending troops to Vietnam was NOT a mistake (71 percent from the age group between ages 21-29).[24] As the number of protestors grew, the percentage of those who agreed with the war waned. In May 1971, only 28 percent of the public supported the war. Thereafter, Gallup stopped asking.

Media bears a huge responsibility for civil unrest. Media, primarily television coverage, invaded our homes and shattered the "rightness" of war most U.S. citizens held since World War II, especially when it came to Communist aggression. Visual exploitation of the blood and guts so intrinsic to war shattered the faith of many Americans. Graphic coverage of casualties eliminated the glory of war concepts embedded in the American psyche. Thus the myths we have written about earlier in this chapter began to take on reality. Americans became divided between the peace movement—the "Doves," and those who sought victory in Vietnam—the "Hawks."

Of the 210,000 men accused of dodging the draft, somewhere in the neighborhood of 30,000 left the country and sought asylum in Canada, Sweden, and Mexico. Of those who chose not to dodge the draft, some got married, some went into the Peace Corp., others joined the National Guard. Veterans Administration statistics show that only 25 percent of the troops serving in combat zones had been drafted (compared to 66 percent during World War II).[25] Most who served on the battlefields had enlisted in the military.

The last of our troops came home from Vietnam in 1973. Conscription ended in 1973. Protests slowed to a drip. The war for the American GI was over. Then why had the divisive issues between society and the warriors not been resolved and laid to rest? Vicious degradation didn't evaporate just because a peace treaty had been signed. For ten years society had done their best to denigrate and vilify the warrior—men who served because they honored their duty to God and country. So rancorous were the protestations that our warriors chose not to enter the fray. Also, remember the veteran served a year in Vietnam. Many came home and shortly thereafter were honorably discharged from the military. They entered society, got a job, raised a family—And shut out the past. Unfortunately, like a smoldering volcano, the pressure grew and, for many, eventually erupted.

In the 1980s the Veterans Administration took seriously the dangers of post-traumatic stress disorder and its kinfolks—traumatic brain injury and secondary traumatic stress. Consequently, the veterans' standing in society took a turn for the better. (For a better understanding of our warriors, we define post-traumatic stress disorder as the seen and unseen manifestation of a disease of the heart and soul of a man or woman sustained on the battlefield and engraved on the psyche and body. The effects of physical and emotional trauma may be treated, and heal, but it leaves scars that are forever apparent to the sufferer and his or her family. PTSD doesn't go away, but it can be managed.)

Summary
Truth—a Hope and a Future

Janett's brother became an alcoholic. She said, "My brother's homecoming was at best nothing, and at worst, ridicule. One can't help but wonder if his homecoming had been more positive, would he have lived a more productive life?"

We can only speculate what might have been. Most assuredly the lies took a decisive toll on the brave men and women who served in our nation's military.

At this point you may question why I bother to speak of the lies, myths, and wannabes—that distant past which like the war itself seems to have faded into history. Or you may wonder why we have spent so much space on defining PTSD. You may question the wisdom of opening old wounds. Many of our beloved warriors found it safer to hide from their wartime experiences and such things as survivors' guilt, flashbacks, and reoccurring nightmares, but such incidents are indelibly written on the veterans' brains and continue to haunt them. Given the right stimuli, the veteran responds physically and emotionally to his military training and his wartime experiences. In the past, many found it easier to "stuff it" than to endure caustic verbal abuse and hateful actions by society and government. But such action may prolong the inevitable. Unchecked trauma will surface. We will look more closely at guilt, flashbacks, and nightmares in later chapters.

In listening to the cries of family members and veterans, we find that "stuffing" it doesn't eradicate it. It has become a cancer multiplying in the cells of our emotions and it may eventually consume and destroy the soul. One would hope that through the aging process the past will indeed be neutralized. However, we think it is more accurate to say that in most cases our perspective more clearly defines the tumultuous issues and the traumatic stress is always there. We may choose to cultivate a new and positive paradigm, but the old paradigm is waiting in the wings for their cue to enter center stage. Furthermore, lies, myths, and wannabes may change their costumes, but they are permanent cast members in the drama of life. The name of the war doesn't change the outcome.

While we speak mostly to veterans of the Vietnam era and their family members, we fear that some things never change. Our returning veterans from the Iraqi and Afghanistan wars may find themselves embroiled in similar circumstances. The lies and myths may differ, but the damage done to the psyche of our warriors may be quite similar. To be aware of the dangers makes us less vulnerable to lifelong traumatic stress and personal and family upheaval. One last thought…

Rumblings Today

Rumblings of war clamor about us. Unlike the disconnection with society and the military in the '60s and '70s, we have an opportunity to support our servicemen and women. We who suffered the war in Vietnam and/or live with the veterans of that savagely maligned war should be vigilant in our support of those currently serving in the armed service and their families. Lies, half-truths, and exaggerations continue to permeate the sound waves pounding our eardrums. Myths are meant to deceive and lies are costly. Verbiage is not cheap and neither is it straightforward. It rings like a "loud gong and a noisy cymbal." It behooves the warriors and families of the '60s and '70s to sift through the rhetoric, find and embrace the truth and those who defend us and all that is good about the United States.

Life is a chain of choices:
That chain will either empower you
or imprison you.
The choice is yours.
Diana Rahe Taylor

CHAPTER 3
Five Archways for Hope and a Future

Our goal for writing about the Vietnam War is not solely to teach history, but to propose some ideas as to how to counter the negative effects of combat experienced by the veteran and the family members, especially the spouse. Therefore, in this chapter we suggest five "archways." May these archways and others to follow be an entrance into a more gratifying future for the family members and their warriors. We are not so naive as to think we can "pen" away the negativity surrounding the war in Vietnam. Rather let us seek to take control of our own thoughts and actions. Our hope is to empower and affirm you, the warrior, and the spouse and family. Our prayer is that we become a beacon of strength to other veterans and their families.

How do I interpret archways? I see it as an egress without gates and doors. Sometimes you travel through and progress for a lengthy distance; other times you retrace your steps and begin again. The goal is to get started and move forward. Second, each archway has a keystone. Webster's Dictionary defines a keystone as, "1) the wedge-shaped piece at the crown of an arch that locks the other pieces in place; 2) something on which associated things depend for support; 3) a species of plant or animal that is considered essential to maintaining the stability of an ecosystem."[26]

As the wife of a warrior—first, we are the "keystone" that holds the family unit together. Second, we "support" to the best of our ability our warriors, our children, and often the extended family members. And, third, we strive to bring "stability" into our homes. Thus the "archway" presents a visual picture of openness and activity. The spouse, the keystone, sustains the arch, keeping the pathway clear for positive forward movement. Let us begin our journey.

First—Love and Respect Yourself

Whether you are the spouse or the warrior, believe in yourself and your choices. We all know that freedom is not free; it is bought with the bravery and the blood of men and women who are called to defend our rights and privilege to live in America. But what, we ask, does it mean to be free?

In 1941, President Franklin Delano Roosevelt delivered his famous State of the Union Address to Congress which has since been accredited for identifying four essential human rights. I believe it laid the groundwork for much of our foreign policies. This same theme was incorporated into the Atlantic Charter and became a significant denominator in the charter of the United Nations. Norman Rockwell captured the essence of FDR's speech in a series of oil paintings known as the "Four Freedoms." They are:

1) The Freedom of Speech, 2) The Freedom of Worship, 3) The Freedom from Want, and 4) The Freedom from Fear.

It would appear that the dissenters of the 1960s and 1970s reaped for themselves the privileges of these four freedoms while they raped these same rights from the veterans, especially the combat veterans who served in Vietnam. It would appear that the Golden Rule—"Do unto others as you would have them do unto you"—did not apply to them. But, we suggest to you, that we who served and who live with those who have served are free to live above their rancor. As my father often said, "Do as I say, not as they do."

We have seen a positive step forward by the Vietnam warriors I have had the privilege of meeting. They are indeed holding their heads high. Statistics tell us that 91 percent of the Vietnam veterans are glad they served and 74 percent said they would serve again, even knowing the outcome.[27]

Had Congress stuck to their promises to financially support the South Vietnamese government, the results may well have been different, but for this discussion, it is a moot point. What is important is for you, the veterans, your spouses, and your family members, to know is this—beyond any doubt you fulfilled with honor your duties. You have every right to be proud of your service. Respect yourself and your fellow servicemen. Wives and families respect and honor their service to this country.

Second—Learn from Mistakes

Let us learn from our own mistakes and from the mistakes of others, even those made by society and government. The Vietnam experience has forced the military to evaluate the needs of the servicemen and, consequently, our military men and women are better prepared and equipped today than were our men and women serving in the Vietnam War. Militarily speaking, we have indeed learned from the Vietnam War. Our men and women in the field today are well trained and better equipped than any who previously served in the armed services.

It took many years and much prodding for the Veterans Administration to listen to the cries of the Vietnam veteran, most especially the combat veteran, but eventually the message was heard. Post-traumatic stress disorder is real and dangerous. Counseling and other programs are more available now and more are coming on board, whether it be mental or physical help, finding a home or a job, or returning to school. Thanks to the Vietnam War, veteran the Veteran's Administration, Vet Centers, and both private and nonprofit organizations are reaching out to all vets.

One of the most significant developments in just the last ten years has been reunions, such as the Mobile Riverine Force Association Reunions and specific unit reunions. These reunions allow vets to connect with other vets. Warriors have learned that they are indeed a Brotherhood. However, we should never underestimate the power of one-on-one meetings—private settings—Brother strengthening Brother.

The question remains then to ask ourselves, have we as a people extrapolated something of worth from the taunting myths and egregious lies of the '60s and '70s? Yes. At the top of the heap—honor the warrior even when we disagree with the politics. Which brings us to the third archway.

Third—Support the Troops and
the Families of Those Serving in the Military today

Not only is today's military well armed and well trained, but it is 100 percent volunteer. Families communicate in ways we who were involved in the Vietnam War never dreamed of. We wrote letters and had reel-to-reel "letter" exchanges—far better communication than those who served in Korea or World War II—but nothing as effective as Skype and other such electronic wizardry. No one wants to be separated. The personal sacrifice our military families make is far greater than anything the average American family has to live with. Technology plays a strategic role in the psychological well-being of our military men and women. Let us be grateful for the progress, but let us not be blinded to the danger lurking in the shadows.

Two intrinsic and potentially tyrannical emotions seem to drive humanity—fear and greed. I think we would agree that the protestors of the '60s and '70's feared they might be called to serve in the war zone, and the best defense was a good offense. They took up verbal arms against the government that had the right to draft them into military service. And the government, primarily our president, wanted to be the hero who stopped the spread of Communism. Keep in mind there were at least three presidents (Kennedy, Johnson, and Nixon) whose decisions strongly influenced the ebb and flow of the Vietnam War.

Forgive me for oversimplifying this very complex arena, but here again, we have learned something. We have learned that we can successfully raise and maintain a 100 percent voluntary armed service. Let us learn to show and speak our appreciation for their service.

I (Diana) am told that the present-day military men and women much prefer to hear, "Thank you for *choosing* to serve."

Fourth—Mend Torn Fences

Rifts between family and friends are painful. Whenever possible, repair the fences and add gates that allow healing and understanding. Nothing could be more compromising to our physical and psychological well-being than unresolved differences. We will explore more of this (i.e. anger and guilt) in the following chapters.

Fifth—Believe in God.

The psalmist of old said,

Blessed is the man who does not walk in the counsel of the wicked, nor stand in the way of the sinner, nor sit in the seat of the mockers. His delight is in the law of the Lord, and on His law he meditates day and night. He shall be like a tree planted by the rivers of water that brings forth its fruit in its season, whose leaf also shall not wither; and whatever he does shall prosper (Psalm 1:1-3).

Our country's first settlers came to this continent seeking freedom to worship a holy God in a manner of their choosing. Our forefathers, most with a firm and personal faith in an eternal God, believed God Himself ordained our existence as a nation. Our laws are based on the Mosaic laws of the Torah. For all intensive purposes, it would appear that a great God has blessed this nation. It behooves us to accept His gift and accept His counsel.

The Great Lady of the Lamp which stands in the New York harbor welcomed millions of desperate souls who hoped for a brighter future. We in this great country have thrown open our arms to "the tired, the poor, and the huddled masses yearning to breathe free." Regardless of the reason our ancestors came to these shores, they came seeking an opportunity to make a better life for themselves, their families, and the generations to come. Many of them left oppressive governments, knowing their providence lay in the hands of loving God and a freedom-loving nation. May our efforts be as valiant and noble.

The psalmist said that he who follows the commands of a just God will prosper. We may not accumulate masses of wealth or find ourselves singing at Carnegie Hall, but we can and are perhaps inclined to recognize and honor the benevolence of the Almighty. It is our belief that when we rest in His care, we find peace within our souls.

When you decide upon a goal,
you override your failure mechanism
and change the direction of your life.
Brian Tracy

CHAPTER 4
Trust

For most Americans the Vietnam War is an event in history, but for some, the war may well have been yesterday or last night. Yes, the bombings and shooting have long since ceased. But we the wives of the Vietnam combat veteran live with the consequences—the psychological, emotional, physical, and relational trauma that bursts into our lives and homes regardless of the calendar day or year. We know that the war lives on in the minds of our warriors. We are often the recipients of their frustration, their anger, their pain, and their numbness. We suffer with them and for them.

JoAnn Moore, wife of Guy P. Moore, knew something was wrong. "Guy, like many combat veterans, suffered from post-traumatic stress—all of it war-related," she said, adding, "I went twenty-nine years not really knowing exactly what was wrong. Guy rarely talked about Vietnam."

Trauma surfaces differently for some. Susan Tuzcu said, "Erol is very impatient and will stop listening or walk away if he has no interest or has lost interest in something. He has gone for weeks without speaking to me for some remark that was misunderstood. He will withdraw into the television. He used to drink until he was no longer conscious."

Why? Why doesn't my warrior confide in me? I (Diana) wonder. Why doesn't he trust me?

Dr. James Johnson says this, "Trust for the combat veteran had begun to vaporize long before returning home. Returning from a year (or less) of a living hell where we saw so many of our Brothers maimed and killed created a paradox of immense proportions in our souls. We went to Vietnam scared but curious and, for the most part, with a feeling that we were going to 'fight for our country.' Once it became clear that we were in reality fighting for our Brothers beside us and that our country was on the other side of the world, without knowing it we began losing our trust."[28]

Just a Bit of History

Four-plus decades ago the United States was seesawing with the Hanoi government at what has been called the Paris Peace Accord. Peace talks stalled over and over again. On March 30, 1972, North Vietnam began another major offensive sweep into South Vietnam on par with the TET offensive that had occurred in February 1968, but this time the smell of success was in the nostrils of the North Vietnamese Army (NVA). The United States responded mid-April 1972 by sending B-52s and U.S. Navy and Air Force bombers to take out supply dumps near Haiphong's harbor and petroleum storage facilities near Hanoi. Protesters in the U.S. went ballistic. They were livid, vocal, and violent. While they demanded the government cease their war efforts, they took the vengeance out on the veterans who had served in Vietnam.

To fully appreciate the significance of the resumed activity, we must remember the U.S. government hoped to push the lagging peace talks to a favorable conclusion—favorable to both the U.S. and South Vietnam. Throughout the year, the Paris Peace talks waxed and waned. Nevertheless, even before the peace treaty was signed, President Nixon promised and proceeded to systematically reduce the American fighting force from Southeast Asia. We should not be surprised to note that the North Vietnamese accelerated their takeover of the South. Yet, on January 27, 1973, the cease-fire was signed and the remaining American troops and a number of prisoners were sent home.

Our withdrawal hung the South Vietnamese government out to dry. To make matters worse for the South Vietnamese Army, Congress voted against further financial and technical aid—a total turnaround from the previous commitments the U.S. had made to them. A reduction of monies that would have supported their military men and supplied necessary equipment crippled whatever chance they may have had to hold off the Communist takeover. Saigon fell in April 1975.

The signing of the Paris Peace Accord in January of 1973 should have been a jubilant occasion for all Americans, but such was not the case for those who served valiantly on the battlefields. Yes, the general public celebrated the cessation of fighting, but God forbid, they should let our warriors forget they were scumbags.

Whatever faith and trust our combat veterans once had in their government and the American populace evaporated on the tarmac when they reached the United States. Yesterday, they carried a weapon and faced life-and-death situations. It was kill or be killed but today… today, they couldn't buy a beer, couldn't vote, and dared not mention they had served the United States of America in Vietnam for fear they would be spit upon or called baby-killers. Is it any wonder these men distrusted politicians and society?

The Vietnam veteran might put his uniform in mothballs, but such would not be the case when it came to his memories. "I was mad at the world," says Terry Gander.

Dave Schoenian has isolated himself to only having friends who are combat veterans. This gave him security. "I stay within my safe zone, which is my base camp," Dave said. "I am still in combat in my mind."[29]

Terry Gander told his wife Donna, "Many Brothers want to, or prefer to, forget Nam ever happened. I, on the other hand, will not, and do not want to ever forget."

Where does that leave us as wives?

"I have to back off and keep my thoughts to myself," said June Carolus.

Barbara Cannode said, "I try to cope, although being human, I'm sure I push his buttons. You would think I would know better."

And Susan Tuzcu admits, "Erol is loving in his own way, but if I expect more, then I will be disappointed."

TRUST—a Coveted Gift

Dr. Jim Johnson said, "Fortunately, some of us have learned to change 'I can never trust anyone about anything' to 'I can trust some people some of the time about some things.'"[30]

Trust, as defined by *Webster's New World College Dictionary*, is "a firm belief or confidence in the honesty, integrity, reliability, justice of another person or thing; faith."

Trust is something one gives to another or places in something such as trust/faith in God. At the heart of trust is truth. That most certainly explains why some combat veterans don't trust most people and certainly not "things" like our government. They feel that society and politicians have either outright lied or twisted or tainted the truth to suit their agendas. From my perspective and from the research I've done, I'd agree they have a point. But, as Dr. Johnson has said, "The warriors' trust melted away long before he got home from the warfront." The question remains—can we bridge the gap and build or rebuild trust? As a wife of a Vietnam warrior, I believe we can and have made inroads into the heart of this issue. One way to do that is for us as wives to alter our paradigm of expectations.

JoAnn Moore said, "Once I understood something about combat trauma, I encouraged Guy to get help."

While the Veterans Administration is not without its problems, they have made great strides to help the veteran suffering from post-traumatic stress. Like JoAnn, we can encourage our warriors to seek help.

"Encourage" is an interesting endeavor. Most of the men I know are not good patients. Even getting them to a doctor or VA hospital takes a bit of ingenuity, but once they get there, they will usually find safe, caring support among veterans who suffer with similar issues. Skilled and experienced counselors are available. Albeit with the returning veterans from Iraq and Afghanistan, the need has multiplied and many more counselors are needed.

Periodically, we take our cars in for new tires that must be realigned and balanced. Building trust is a bit like getting new tires. Terry Gander said he doesn't want to forget what happened in Vietnam. My husband, Charlie Taylor, feels the same. But what I hope we can do is realign and balance the emotions that accompany the memories. It's perspective. It may well begin with us—the wives—as we search for our own personal growth and understanding.

Another thing that has helped today is a more amiable society. Quite often, I've heard "Joe Citizen" say to a Vietnam veteran, "Thanks for your service." On one occasion, a woman got up from her seat in a restaurant and greet Charlie with, "Welcome home." We were on cloud nine the remainder of the day and it has instilled more positive thoughts ever since. I stand amazed at the power those two words brought into our lives, especially for Charlie.

Charlie and I have noticed in more recent times that more and more Vietnam veterans are identifying themselves by wearing baseball caps that say "Vietnam Veteran." We've decided that for the most part the veteran has come to grips with his participation in the war—a war he can say he proudly fought. "Statistics tell us that 91 percent of Vietnam veterans say they are glad they served. And, 74 percent say they would serve again even knowing the outcome."[31] War is hell and hell is not a pretty place, but if you've been there, be proud you served and honor those who did not make it home.

We as a nation continue to be embroiled in foreign wars and a host of hotspots across the globe. I have no doubt we have some dissenters in our population, but few are as vocal as those in the 1970s. Thank the Lord! Those who served in Vietnam can and should claim their honor. It is long overdue and greatly needed.

One of the most gratifying spin-offs from military reunions is unity, often referred to as "Brotherhood." Harmony, compatibility, rapport, and a host of other adjectives just begin to define this awesome relationship. It crosses barriers like no other homogeneous group.

Susan Tuzcu said Erol went to his first reunion without her, but with a fellow combat veteran. The next time they went, he wanted Susan to go.

I remember our first reunion—the Army/Navy Riverine Force Association Reunion in Kentucky. Fearing it would be too overwhelming, Charlie took a book with the thought he would escape to the hotel room and hide. He left me in the room and ventured to the gathering. Hours passed. Combing the halls looking for him, I stepped into a number of rooms, including the main banquet room. Then I found him. He was deep in conversation and while I think he knew I sat down beside him, he never looked my way. I eventually went back to the room, puzzled and pleased by his total involvement with the group. It was as if he had found his home after being lost for years. I came and went several times. Late in the evening I went to bed. I didn't see him again until the wee hours of the morning. His behavior and that of his comrades is normal and natural. It's Brotherhood!"

Allow me to share with you a more recent story which demonstrates the strength of the Brotherhood bond. Charlie and I were in Vietnam in December 2011. We went to the shores of the Rach Ba Rai river, known as "Snoopy's Nose" because the curvature of the river reminded them of this wonderful cartoon character. A major battle starting early in the morning and lasting throughout the day and into the night had occurred on this river bend on September 15, 1967. When the smoke cleared the following day, seven Americans had been killed and 123 had been wounded. Fast forward to December 2011. Of all the places, battlefields, base camps, and the like that we traveled to see in Vietnam, this spot remained with few changes. The emotions of the warriors within our tour group were tangible.

After our trip home, I reported our findings and emotions to the women who are part of this team. In response, I received this note from Terry Gander (wife—Donna) who had fought for his life and the lives of his comrades at "Snoopy's Nose" on September 15, 1967. He said, "I am now wondering what it would be like for me to walk along the very banks of the Rach Ba Rai river as Charlie did. Perhaps someday I will find out. Please give Charlie my best...I tell ya...I just love the guy." Charlie responded, "I love you too."

That's Brotherhood. It spans the passage of time and embraces shared hardships. Forty years doesn't erase their memories or minimize the horrors of that horrific experience. It enriches and solidifies relationships. Brotherhood—unity of heart and soul. Nothing could be finer or more welcomed.

Trust brings with it an element of stability and sincerity. Combat is anything but predictable; consequently, the warrior learns distrust from the get-go. Pam Roger's quiet confidence and sincerity has helped Terry Gander (Pam's brother-in-law) to build trust and respond to her questions. Pam, Donna, and their brother have been instrumental in bringing stability and sincerity into Terry's life.

Sally C. became aware of her husband's Vietnam experience months after they were married. "I wondered why he did not tell me earlier," she said. "I was amazed by his raw emotions, but now we are older and wiser. We can talk about his wartime encounters. Recently he has gotten interested and proud to be a veteran of the Vietnam War."

I sense a sincere resolve behind her words as she seems to be saying, "We can do this together." And so she bridged the arroyo between trust and distrust with tenacity and love.

To build trust, one must be tractable—amenable, submissive, willing to climb out and away from one paradigm and adapt a new one. This is one of the areas where counseling plays a big role. I am best acquainted with the Alcoholics Anonymous program because I have a son who has abused substances, and I'm glad to say he has been sober for over twenty years. We have dear friends who are in AA programs. One of its strengths is honest evaluations and a willingness to change and accept reality. A strong component of this program is *The Serenity Prayer* written by Reinhold Niebuhr. This simple guideline has the power to turn reality on its ear. It helps us focus our thoughts to truth and manageable actions. You may recognize the first three lines. I have used them many times to help me when I need to make a decision, pleasant or unpleasant as the case may be.

God grant me the serenity to accept the things I cannot change;
Courage to change the things I can;
And wisdom to know the difference.

These phrases have the power to change your life 180 degrees. Less known, but equally powerful is the rest of the prayer:

Living one day at a time;
Enjoying one moment at a time;
Accepting hardships as the pathway to peace.
Taking, as He did, this sinful world as it is, not as I would have it;
Trusting that He will make all things right if I surrender to His will;

That I may be reasonably happy in this life and
Supremely happy with Him forever in the next.
Amen.

Please find a copy of this prayer and sear it on your brain and in your heart. It may add balance and purpose to your future. Better still, paste a copy of it on your bathroom mirror so you can absorb its power every day.

I'm the Spouse—How Do I Build Trust?

The great apostle Paul wrote about love, saying it was the greatest act and emotion known to God and mankind. In 1 Corinthians 13 (known as the love chapter of the Bible), Paul writes: "Love never fails. Love is kind and is patient. It is not self-seeking and it does not keep records of wrongs." Could anything be more simplistic to read and yet so difficult to put into practice?

Many of the women I've talked to and most of our team will tell you that it is not easy to love a traumatized combat veteran. They can be grumpy, angry, sometimes dangerous, and silent and morose. Sometimes they cry. Emotions and actions often are volatile and unpredictable. Some of our team members have had experience in one or more of these issues. Most are committed to bringing healing within the hearts of their warrior. Is it easy? No, it is not. Are we 100 percent successful? No, but we all are striving forward and praying for success and wholeness. Perhaps this compilation of our experiences may be helpful with similar circumstances.

Working first with the easier-said-than-done ideas, here are some basic rules for engaging our warriors in conversation.

1. Obtain permission to ask questions regarding the warrior's year in combat. Then listen. Recognize that some experiences will never be shared and other things will be shared at some later date.

2. Fixing a problem may require time and patience and may be better left for a counselor to handle. For most of our warriors, it is not about "fix"; it's all about being heard and respected.

3. Don't be a timekeeper. Give of your time freely and exclusively, if at all possible without interruptions. If there are children in

the home, sharing will be narrow windows usually after the children are in bed.

4. Answer only when asked for an answer. This will be rare and, in some cases, may be advisable in the presence of a counselor.
5. Don't make promises you cannot keep. Remember, one of the frail characteristics of the combat veteran is the lack of trust. A lie or a perceived untruth may obliterate future discussions. Resurrecting trust is a lifetime journey.

The following poem was written by June Marie Carolus whose husband, Jim, served two tours with the Marines in Vietnam. The poem encapsulates the need and desire most of our warriors feel for a listening partner—one they can trust.

LISTEN TO ME

Listen to me and what do you hear,
A troubled soldier it is perfectly clear.
I changed my life to keep others free,
But no one has time to think of me.
Even though I chose to pay the cost,
I now wander through life feeling lost.
Others don't hear my plea for peace,
A fractured mind I wish to cease.

Listen to me the thoughts come slow,
As the battle within me continues to grow.
My pride is tattered and torn from defeat,
Dark secrets are kept I don't dare repeat.

The pain won't dissolve within my soul,
A no-win situation out of control.
The guilt hovers daily it tackles my heart,
Why my life is spared while others depart.

Listen to me the tears form and fall,
Flashbacks come often of that fatal call.
A shell of a man I have become,
From misunderstood sacrifices of all not some.

I sit in a chair my back to the wall,
Watching who enters from down the hall.
My paranoia lingers though counseling I seek,
The future of my turmoil seems very bleak.

Listen to me you will soon learn the rest,
Post-traumatic stress disorder is put to the test.
A mission persuaded to give up the past,
Etched reflections as such just won't let it last.

June Marie Carolus.

Trust Is a Journey

As I contemplate the message of this chapter and the message I want to instill in your heart, it is this: Trauma happens, but TRUST can bring healing. Building TRUST is a bit like basic training. The making of a warrior is a process that comes with time and training. Building TRUST can begin the arduous process toward healing from the traumatic experience of war. TRUST is like the siding and roof of a home built on a foundation of love and truth. TRUST is a protective shield for all that is invaluable to us—our hearts and our homes. TRUST will enrich our lives and our marriages. TRUST yourself. TRUST your spouse. And let us remember this—a building built with quality materials will stand the wear and tear of time.

In Conclusion

Nothing speaks more succinctly of TRUST than parachuting. I had the privilege of sitting across the table discussing parachuting with Dan Galde who was a pararescueman in the Air Force and operated as such in North and South Vietnam, Laos, Thailand, and Cambodia in 1967–70. He went on to retire from the military. Dan was not only a Master parachutist, but also an instructor and flight examiner. He graciously corrected my vocabulary and misconceptions about jumping. Over and over he would say, "A parachute is to the paratrooper what the weapon and comrades are to the foot soldier."

When speaking with Dan about parachuting, he commented on the uncertainty of the landing. "Landing zones are the only uncontrollable element in parachuting," he said. "All other components are micro-managed by highly trained and experienced parachutists."

I wish the same could be said about the combat veterans. Returning after their tour in Vietnam, they jumped without a fully functioning parachute into a society that failed them miserably.

In 1997, Charlie and I went sky diving. We placed 100 percent of our trust in the reliability of the parachute, the pilot, and the crew regulating the jumps. Parachuting involves the coordination and cooperation of dozens, if not hundreds, of people. It is all- encompassing; every step in the process, from the training to the landing, must be managed to perfection. Precision or lack of it will make or break a successful jump.

First, the parachute must be packed properly or it will not open sufficiently to allow it to inflate and both store and resist air. If it does not open properly, it will not sustain the body weight of the jumper, and the ensuing crash will be devastating or deadly. Second, parachuting is about taking the great leap of faith, leaving the airplane for the wide spaces of sky—when it's just you and the chute on a destiny with the earth. Third, the pilot, the plane, and the crew play a vital part in the process. Every step in the process must be executed with precision. It is a matter of life and death.

If the chute, the plane, and all those who make jumping a safe event aren't operating well, no one will enjoy or survive the jump. Walking and working toward healing from PTS/PTSD is a process that begins and grows with TRUST—working together, in tandem with family, friends, and medical professionals—hoping, praying, and planning for wholeness in our journey through life.

If I speak God's Word with power,
Revealing all his mysteries and
Making everything plain as day,
And if I have faith that says to a mountain,
"Jump," and it jumps, but I don't love, I'm nothing."
1 Corinthians 13:2 (*The Message*)

CHAPTER 5
PTSD—Post-Traumatic Stress Disorder

Sharing her experience, Barbara Bedell writes, "My brother, Craig Bedell, was in the 11th Armored Cavalry. He was injured when first arriving in Vietnam and was made a supply clerk for the majority of his time there. Toward the end of his tour he was deemed combat ready and sent out during very heavy fighting. He saw more than I think he was capable of processing in that short time. He returned from Vietnam as someone else. He wasn't the brother I had before he left. He wasn't able to talk about his experiences there. He returned in August 1969 and died in a car accident in July 1975. I feel he was just as much a victim of the war as anyone who died in battle. He never received any help. He didn't and still doesn't count. I feel like he was just thrown away by the military. I think if he had never gone to Vietnam, he would still be here today."

A friend recently shared a similar story. Janett said, "My brother who served in Vietnam was one of the walking wounded. His physical wounds healed but the mental wounds only intensified as he grew older. Like many he self-medicated with alcohol. When he finally sought help, he had severe alcoholic problems, and they stayed with him the rest of his life. He died a few years ago."

PTSD—What Is It?

They called it shell shock in World War I and battle fatigue in World War II.

We now know it as PTSD—post-traumatic stress disorder. Call it by whatever name suits you, but understand the trauma is real, not a myth, and it never goes away. The term post-traumatic stress disorder came into our vocabulary during the 1980s, and from our point of view best describes the effect of war on the psyche of the warrior. War sucks the goodness and peace from a person's soul and robs him or her of normal, psychological development.

Terry Gander said, "I was at the end of the line, the end of my rope. I could not deal with this thing that was wrong with me…because I didn't know what it was in the first place. Fortunately I simply broke down mentally and spent seven days in a mental institution. Then my doctor told me that my insurance company wanted me out of the institution and sent to the VA where I could get my treatments free. At the VA I was immediately diagnosed with PTSD and began weekly treatments as an outpatient. That is what I meant by making that statement (above). If it had not been for the treatments…I'm sure I would have ended it all. Thank God I didn't and that's what I'm thankful for. I honestly do not think I would have survived to this time in my life without the proper care and treatment."

I can't begin to tell you how much I appreciate Terry. He is a true hero. His transparency and honesty about his pain and his journey ministers and instructs all of us. His life and his message speak the truth with hope and compassion. He and the men and women who have contributed to this book have "taken point." They go before us pioneering the VA system and exploring treatments which may benefit warriors past and present. With outstretched arms of welcome and understanding, they encourage all who are hurting from PTSD or Secondary PTSD to embrace healing.

Terry Gander, and all of the men who have been interviewed, are true heroes. We are grateful for their dedicated service during the Vietnam War. We salute their assistance in writing this book and Dr. Johnson's previously published book—*Combat Trauma* in which he writes:

"Today the VA is considerably more progressive and active in offering treatment and assistance to veterans than it was in years past.

We certainly know that the VA system, both medically and administratively, has been stretched, and this no doubt has created delays and in some cases degraded service and treatment."[32]

When Terry Gander made his initial statement to Dr. Johnson for the book on *Combat Trauma*, he said, "Now that PTSD has been recognized by the VA, many vets are receiving medical care not previously available. I honestly do not think I would have made it through to this time in my life without the proper care and treatment. For this, I am extremely grateful."[33]

JoAnn Moore said of her husband: "Guy retired in 2004 after working many years 12-14 hour days and often weekends. When he retired, he was suddenly alone with his head. He became very difficult to live with. Not just me, but friends and family noticed. It was then he found out about the meetings for veterans. He learned about the VA hospital in Chicago. It was there that he got treatment. Did it work 100 percent? No, but it helped a lot."

In a symposium I was privileged to attend, I found a vast array of support groups approaching the vets' needs from various angles—housing, jobs, education, etc. Most of these groups are nonprofit organizations and not part of the Veterans Administration System. Some of these groups are national in scope, some are local. There seemed to be a healthy connection with the VA system. All looked for ways to support and improve the servicemen's needs.

In Conclusion

It's September 2014 and recent news gives the VA system a failing grade. I would agree that while the VA is far from perfect, it has made great strides over the last few years. And yes, there is room for improvement. We can only hope that the press has forced their hand and we will see greater improvements in the near future.

In the meantime, local and national nonprofit organizations are assisting with the physical and material needs of our veterans. Vet Centers have provided counseling through individual and group settings. I (Diana) believe the bad press will spur action and improvements will be coming on a variety of levels—nationally and locally.

It is my hope and prayer that as we put our words into action we will be able to reach out to men like Craig Bedell and Janett's brother who have been severely traumatized by war. While we have failed some, others have been helped, and more will be helped in the future.

Suppose I give everything I have to poor people.
And suppose I give my body to be burned.
If I don't have love,
I get nothing at all.
1 Corinthians 13:3

CHAPTER 6
Guilt - "Why him and not me?"

Dave Schoenian remembers the day God spared him. "I had just traded places with another soldier who wanted to fire the machine gun on the boat if we were ambushed. When the rockets hit the boat he took the blast in front of me; his leg was just about blown off and many others were wounded. Why him and not me?"[34]

"I frequently think of all the good men who died in Nam and yet I made it home (Roy Moseman)."[35]

Mitchell Perdue said, "If I had continued to walk point, Yount's bullet would have been for me. If I hadn't gone to the aid of our medic, Campbell's bullet would have also been for me."

Mitch Perdue passed away September 9, 2009. Jim Johnson said, "A few days prior to his death, Mitch and I shared some reflections of our lives' journey. We both knew he had only a very short time to live. With all his family at his bedside, we laughed, reminisced, and made an agreement that whichever of us got to heaven first would find a peaceful 'heavenly' stream. When the second arrives, we will gather on the quiet stream banks with our other combat Brothers and share the peace of eternity—but with no enemy snipers, booby traps, ambushes, gunboats, choppers, C rations, or that god-awful leg-sucking mud.

"Our chains of physical and emotional wounds often places us in the category of feeling guilty when we see how badly our Brothers had it who were dismembered and/or lost their lives. Our guilt often trans-formed into other feelings and became fuel sources for anger, sadness, and even fear that others would not understand—and they probably don't," Dr. Johnson writes.[36]

"Guilt is an unpleasant feeling. Unresolved guilt however, keeps memories emotionally charged and in active memory," Dr. Glenn Schiraldi writes,[37] adding, "Grief is the normal response to loss. "Grieving is about finding our way again."[38]

After numerous conversations with combat veterans, I (Diana) have come to the conclusion that feelings of guilt fall into three main categories, and yes, they overlap at times. Guilt may stem from a myriad of causes, but I've narrowed it to three which I believe covers much of the combat veterans' pain.

First, and primary in almost all cases, is **survivor guilt**. Why did one warrior die and another live? God alone knows the answer to this heart-wrenching question that plagues so many veterans. Second, is what I've come to think of as **the moral conflict**. Why do innocent people (noncombatants) die or get wounded? And third, **occupational hazards**. When does a warrior's reflexive duty and training present a danger to troops and civilians? It's the old what if, woulda, coulda, and shoulda game with which they flagellate themselves.

First—A Look at Survival Guilt

Perhaps most common to combat veterans is this debilitating sense of survival guilt. A Brother died and the warrior wonders why him and not me? It leaves the warrior with feeling guilty for being alive. Such was the case for Terry Gander.

When I asked Donna, wife of Terry, about this guilt which burdens him, she said, "Guilt—yes, for leaving some Brothers behind in Nam and not being able to properly grieve their loss. He feels guilty for being able to come home to his family, when many other died and could not."

"The only productive work Guy P. Moore could find when he returned from Vietnam was in an auto plant," Jim Johnson writes. "Many years on a career progression that began to reverse itself brought back many bad feelings of combat for Guy."[39]

Speaking for himself, Guy P. Moore says, "The company decided to eliminate my job and put me back on a job I had twenty years prior, on the assembly line. I had to retire because my mental health could not deal with the rejection and demotion. I had a lot of anxiety, irritable mood swings, homicidal and suicidal thoughts, high blood pressure, severe headaches, stomach problems as well as a resurrection of survivor guilt from Vietnam. I don't really know why, but I kept having thoughts of my combat times. I had horrible feelings that I was going over the edge and no sense of future. I didn't care much about anything, especially myself."[40]

JoAnn Moore, Guy's wife, said, "He still feels guilty that he didn't die there and wonders why. He felt so many of the others were a better person than him so why did they die and not him?"

Within this category of guilt, I have included a "modesty or embarrassment" that some combat veterans have toward their medals. It could have fit under the third category—duty bound/duty performed. Some men feel uncomfortable about the medals they were awarded for bravery. In some cases the event being awarded had cost the lives of their comrades. The eternal question, "Why did I survive and they die?" haunts the decorated warrior. Two men whose deeds earned them accommodations were Terry Balfe and Bill S.

Wishing to show her admiration for her husband's heroic service, Marianne ordered Bill's medals with plans to frame them, but Bill couldn't bring himself to look at them. He said, "I didn't want to have to look at them every day of my life and have them bring back memories I've tried to bury. They don't mean anything. A lot of guys did more than I did."

Terry Balfe carries similar guilt with him. He didn't even want his Silver Star mentioned for years and years because he felt he didn't deserve it. He especially questioned why he and not so many others whom he thought had done far braver things didn't receive medals.

Barbe, Terry's wife, said, "When I ask why he hates to be called brave," he laughs and says, 'Hell, I was only trying to stay alive.'

"The other night an Army buddy emailed his appreciation to Terry for his bravery and that he deserved the Silver Star. Terry said, 'It makes me feel *sad* that my fellow comrades feel that way.'"

"Why sad?" I asked him. "He couldn't explain it."

Second—Moral Conflict

Guilt riddles the heart and mind of the warrior and it rarely dissipates, regardless of the passing of time. An article authored by Gregg Zoroya entitled "Study suggests feelings of guilt are a top PTSD cause," was published by *USA Today*. Mr. Zoroya wrote, "A leading cause of post-traumatic stress disorder is guilt that troops experience because of moral dilemmas faced in combat according to preliminary findings of a study of active-duty Marines." Moral injury brings a new dimension to the psychiatrist who work with veterans suffering from PTSD. Diagnostic criteria would "include feelings of shame and guilt," says David Spiegel, a member of the working group rewriting the PTSD section.[41]

The most common cause of moral conflict falls upon the innocent non-combatant, especially the child. Dr. Johnson remembers one tragic event:

"I recall her as a little 'rag doll.' On the night of December 30, 1967, while I was with Company A, the adjoining company called in an artillery marking round. At daybreak the next morning, an old 'papasan' (Vietnamese male) brought a small girl cuddled limply in his arms. She was wrapped in an old blanket, covered with blood. We saw that she had a massive head and face wound. In looking at this small child then and even now, it is all I could or can do to keep from crying. I can still hear the gurgling in her little throat as she fought for breath.

"The image of that broken and disfigured face is still very vivid to me, I don't even know if that once beautiful, black-headed child lived or not. At least we medevaced her, but even if she lived, she would have been disfigured for life."[42]

Ron Miriello has some guilt for accidental machine gun firing on the other side of a jungle which resulted in civilian deaths—this might well be the one thing that haunts him the most, says his wife, Debbie.

Roy Moseman agrees. "A soldier threw a grenade into a bunker shortly after a firefight, believing some VC were in the bunker. When Roy Moseman looked into the bunker, he saw the heart-stopping sight of a little girl about three or four years old who had had her foot blown off. Sad visions of that awful scene are often in Roy's dreams." [43]

Roy adds, "I frequently think of all the good men who died in Nam and yet I made it home. I even think about the VC whom I killed, who had families and children just like we had."[44]

In early 1968, Fire Base Jaeger was hard hit by the VC. One hundred fifty VC were killed and one was captured. Twenty US troops were killed in action and seventy-plus were wounded. Jerry Greenwood, who served with the 5/60 Infantry, B Company in Vietnam and was at Jaeger, said, "Some of the things stuck in my head plagued me. Such things, as the VC whom we buried at Jaeger, still unsettle me. These men had families just like we did. I was relieved when I read Lee Alley's Book, *After the War: Finding Hope and Understanding in Life After Combat*,[45] and found someone other than me had felt guilty when thinking about them."

Third—Reflexive Duty Calls

On the battlefield the warrior does what he has been trained to do. He responds in a split second under fire. These instinctive movements taught during basic and advance training have become part and parcel in the warrior's thoughts and innate muscle responses and are designed to save his when all hell breaks loose on the field of battle. When he is in training, these functions are hypothetical enactments, but on the battlefield they are electrifying reality. Unfortunately, reality has an unpalatable aftertaste that last for the rest of the warrior's life.

Dan Galde, a USAF pararescueman, speaks of times when whether to shoot or not demands an instant decision. He remembers when he and his crew had rescued a downed pilot. Bullets pelted the helicopter. He instinctively returned fire and wiped out the threat, but in so doing, he could have endangered his support crew in planes flying in tandem as backup protection for the rescue team. It was a risk he had not considered when he was in the heat of the moment.

"When someone is firing at you, the decision to return fire is based on kill or be killed. You shoot to protect yourself and your comrades. But," Dan said, "should I shoot a farmer who is plowing his field and toting a gun on his back?" Dan well remembers such an event and still ponders what he should have done.

"Tranquility can easily erupt into a deadly threat. In that case, the picture may not be so black and white. It is times like these that saddle the warrior with guilt—not necessarily at that moment, but hours later, even years later." Dan shared several stories with me (Diana) that still haunt him.

Barbara Cannode, wife of Daniel, said much the same thing. "I hardly think the guilt ever goes away of why them and not me? Why should I have been spared? The *what* did I do, and *why* did we have to do it, even tougher. If asked he would go back without hesitation. He loves his country and everything it stands for. I think not talking about the war is denial enough. Perhaps it is just a horrible nightmare and we will wake up soon."

While some suffer intensely from war-related guilt, others are able to compartmentalize it. Firing into heavy foliated jungle, hooches, or enemy bunkers is a necessary part of war—not pleasant, anything but, but necessary if we are going to stay alive.

Susan Tuzcu feels her husband, Erol, doesn't suffer from guilt per se, because he felt he had a job to do in Vietnam and he did it. However, Susan believes he feels a deep sense of remorse.

My husband, Charlie Taylor, lost a number of his men in combat. However, I have often heard him say he is thankful that he never lost a man because he did something stupid or used bad tactics. Still, one does not lose a comrade, a "Brother," without great sadness—a sadness that reaches across the years.

Dr. James Johnson said, "Right-thinking people feel guilty when things happen that cause regret, remorse, or sadness that the event(s) happened. In combat, these events happened almost daily. Four decades later, numerous events still ring in our minds that cause guilt, even when we may have had nothing to do with the event."[46]

Archway –

Build Strong and Enduring Friendships

Especially Within Your Marriage

A reminder – the "archway" is the egress on our journey through life. That which created the arch and sustained the pressures of the pillars is known as the "keystone." Within this book will be several "Archways"—suggestions on how to stimulate and improve the relationships between the warrior and the spouse. The spouse is the keystone and thus makes possible the egress.

Several wives have said that the husbands they sent to Vietnam were not the same person when they returned home, but because they had made a commitment, they stayed the course. Some married after their warriors returned from war. All of us have had a few surprises along the way. Some warriors, to put it bluntly, have been difficult to live with. We cannot change the past, but we can adjust our thinking and perhaps influence the future.

Not all of the women who have participated in the development of this book have beautiful marriages. Some are divorced. Some of those have remarried. Many of us have been married for a number of years. Some, like Daniel and Barbara, Bill and Marianne, and Terry and Barbe have been married over forty years. The Johnsons and Taylors have celebrated over fifty years. Let us encourage each other to strengthen our friendships within our marriages regardless of our circumstances. And let us commit to building bonds with friends and family, young and old.

On my desk is a greeting card which clearly defines true friendship:
"A person can hear; but a friend listens for the meaning.
A person can look, but a friend sees the heart.
A person can know, but a friends understands your dreams."[47]

A friend is one who weeps with us when the burdens are great and rejoices with us when our joy bubbles over. May our friends be many and our friendships rich and rewarding. Such is our prayer and hope for all who read this book. (More on "Friendships" in Chapter 11.)

Love is patient.

Love is kind.

It does not want what belongs to others.

It does not brag.

It is not proud.

1 Corinthians 13:4

CHAPTER 7
Grief—Haunting, Unrelenting Sorrow

"Recently I (Jim Johnson) was in Washington, DC taking my nine-year-old granddaughter to see the sights. Included were Arlington, the changing of the guard and The Wall. As I was leaving The Wall, another vet came up to me, hugged me and welcomed me home. (I had on my 9th Infantry Div Cap.) He had tears in his eyes, and I asked if he'd been here before. He said no, but he found his three "Brothers" on The Wall.

"Then, I sat on a bench with my wife and granddaughter between The Wall and the Lincoln Memorial for a few moments. Four girls in junior high (14-years-old) from Ohio came up to me and asked if I was a veteran. (I had on my hat). They presented me with an ink pen appropriately inscribed to veterans. They were looking for vets to thank.

"My thank you to them included something like, 'I accept this in behalf of my buddies whose names are on this wall.' One of the girls asked how many of my friends' names were there. I replied, 'Ninety-six. They were the soldiers from the 3/60th Infantry who were killed during my eight-and-a-half-months assignment.'

"With that said, one of the girls suddenly burst out crying uncontrollably. The other three also had tears. It was like suddenly, these were not just names on the wall, they had been real persons. My granddaughter, who is adopted from Guatemala, absorbed all this quietly. Later, she had many questions and comments about the whole series of events.

"I say all this to say that it took me about 36 hours or so after leaving The Wall to emotionally feel back to normal. I was really preoccupied with all my s***."

Charlie Taylor said, "I have stood at the Vietnam Wall Memorial on several occasions. Each name represents a Brother. Each has a family or a friend that mourns their passing. As I stood before that glassy, black wall, and looked at my reflection behind the names, I remind myself that my name could have been there. While I am most fortunate that I am not, I grieve for the loss of my Brothers."

GRIEF—Pain that Never Goes Away

If guilt is a poison that pollutes a stream, killing the fish and vegetation as it flows through the terrain, then grief is the eddy in which the pollution settles. It stagnates. Pollution blinds us to our inner strength. Unless we grieve properly, guilt will become master of our future. It will stymie our forward progression through life. Somewhere within our core we must find a way or a thing that will purify and nourish our souls and hearts.

June Carolus, whose husband, Jim, served two tours with the Marines in Vietnam, said, "He carries a lot of guilt with him. He lived while his friends died and he doesn't understand why. He says if he told me the things that happened over there I wouldn't love him." Jim grieves over the loss of comrades.

June shares this poem that expresses her grief:

Shattered Tears

Home from where it all began
Numbness creeps in from all sides
Compassion is buried from pain within
Heartache brings an emptiness that cannot be filled.

Staring fixed upon a past bears regrets
Hollow thoughts become instilled with blankness
Emotions overflow with guilt, still lingering
A once strong spirit badly beaten subsides.

Tears spill from within, negligent of thought
Anger takes a front seat to pity
Lives and minds collide, at an intersection of the soul
Grief alerts the senses of depression to react.

June Carolus 7/7/2012

The dictionary defines grief as a deep sorrow, sadness, or distress. Just reading Jim's comments to June saddens me. I can only imagine his crushing guilt and grief, a pain that pours into his daily routine and into his marriage. June too suffers. She is not alone. Many wives strain to understand what this terrible monster is that poisons their happiness. Once again, this highlights that PTSD is a family wound.

Most, if not all of us, entered marriage vowing to love, cherish, and obey in sickness and in health, for richer or for poorer, until death parts us. We embraced our mates with stars in our eyes and dreams in our hearts. Keeping that dream alive takes a lot of effort, and for the wife of a combat veteran, it demands a lot of grit. Some marriages didn't make it, not because they didn't put forth the effort or have grit, but simply because…God knows what. He alone knows the secrets of our hearts and minds. Let Him be the judge. Let all of us seek and speak of the journey to healing and endurance.

Becoming "married" is a lot like becoming a parent. We think we know what marriage is all about until we've been married a few months. We think we know what it means to be a father or a mother until we have a child who has a mind of its own and whose ways usurp our authority. For years marriage and parenting are experimental. Then one day we think we have the answer only to find that it can be wrong.

As mentioned earlier, Charlie shipped off to Vietnam just prior to our third wedding anniversary. The man who came home at the end of the year was not the same man I sent off. His moments of grief were sheltered underneath his facade of quiet strength. He didn't rant but often withdrew into his private world. I thought I had lady luck wrapped around my little finger. I was wrong.

Recently he snuggled into his recliner and spent the day mourning.

By evening he was so down, nothing I could do or say seemed to help. He had simply grieved his way throughout the daylight hours, then at dusk he took a sleep-aid and fell into his bed and oblivion. The next day, he tucked his emotions and his grief into his hip pocket and drove off to work and his other world. I, on the other hand, battled sadness until I could lift my head and arms around him upon his return from work. Our world had righted itself—for now.

Barbara Cannode said, "Daniel and I were married in April of '69, two weeks before Dan left for Vietnam. He spent sixteen days less than one year in Vietnam and arrived home four days before our first anniversary. He brought home with him a life of PTSD and we have struggled, fought, sometimes succeeded, got up and fallen down again with our battle together. We are now married over forty years. I often feel hurt and sad. I am angry with our government for taking this wonderful young man I married and sending home to me someone I did not know. Gone is our tender relationship and in its place— confusion as to what to do and how to handle things. And yes, I am damn mad."

Grief may be a thief that cheats the warrior of his personal dignity. It is real and forever with the veteran. It is a permanent reminder of his past experiences with loss, loss of Brothers and loss of innocence. Unfortunately, grief is rarely a solo operation; it spills easily and disrupts the family's tranquility.

Five Stages of Grief

Grief is about loss. For the warrior, loss may be the death of a Brother or loss of one's innocence. Many years ago, a very caring psychiatrist Dr. Elizabeth Kubler-Ross made famous what now is often referred to as the five stages of grief. What Dr. Kubler-Ross and others have said is that grief must take its course. These stages are:

- Denial—No one wants to accept death. And yes, the warrior has seen more than his share of death, the death of a Brother and the loss of his own innocence.
- Anger—Ever present for the warrior is the eternal question, "Why?" We will look at anger in the warrior more fully in chapter 6.

- Bargaining—We might say…If we can make a deal with what life, I'd… If we had… If God would… If I would have done… We cannot roll back the clock, but we would willingly make the outcome different if we could.
- Depression—We will examine depression in a later chapter. Depression brings feelings of hopelessness and can lead to self-pity and bitterness.
- Acceptance—Acceptance is not the same as resignation. Acceptance says the person or event is gone, and it was not my fault.

Grief is difficult and the length of time one grieves has no bearing for the sufferer. Grief is a journey from shock, and in some cases numbness, through fear and depression, and finally to understanding or acceptance. The movement, not necessarily in order, is generally forward but relapses are common.

I know that not all grief can be packaged and tied with a bow. I know because four very important family members have passed from my life. I grieve differently for each of them. I know that certain dates on the calendar will throw me into a tizzy and moments of sorrow and regrets are overwhelming. No, it's not an easy road. For the combat veteran it's a trauma that reaps intrusive abstractions from the heart and the head.

It's also a journey for the spouse of a combat veteran. Each step of the warrior's journey is tenuous for the spouse. One downtime differs from the next down-time. Sometimes it's anyone's guess as to how we should respond, but here are a few hints worth trying.

One, put our own emotions on hold. Avoid reactionary responses.

Two, listen with our hearts as well as our ears. Back in the letter writing days, we would have said, "Read between the lines." After a few stops and starts, it should become clear whether to communicate or remain quiet.

Three, be kind to yourself as well as your warrior.

Grief—Help and Healing

Dealing with grief is like living in a cave. It's dark, it's lonely, and it's horribly uncomfortable. Let me suggest two archways which lead away from the cave and into the wide open spaces. But first, a reminder—archways provide an egress to a future filled with hope and joy. Archways offer practical ways to bring healing into our lives as wives as "keystones" of warriors.

Archway—

First Things First—Counseling

Do not underestimate the power and devastation of grief and its role in Secondary Traumatic Stress (STS/STSD). It is a real and ever-present possibility, our first archway leads us toward counseling. Let me strongly suggest you find a good counselor –someone who can walk with you through the grieving process and give you a workable perspective on guilt.

Grief counseling/therapy helps people cope with loss. While I strongly recommend professional counseling/therapy, I recognize that not all women (spouses) have the financial means for seeking professional help. The Veterans Administration, Vet Centers, and the like are waking up to the need of the spouse and family of warriors suffering from PTSD. Seeking help from these venues should be our first line of help. Churches sometimes offer counseling/therapy services. Since I am speaking mostly to women, let me encourage all of us to find a woman within our acquaintances who is gifted with wisdom and seek her counsel. And yes, many times a good friend is our best resource.

I stress here, however, that not all "friends" give wise counsel. Most friends strengthen us emotionally, but not all friends have counseling and listening skills. A good counselor listens and helps us find ways to cope with our spouses' guilt and grief. Wise friends are often a good resource for helping us navigate the troubled waters in our own lives. A counseling friend walks beside us, listens, and instructs. Often their instruction leads us to our own solutions. A counseling friend directs, but is not controlling.

I have several friends who listen and advise me. With them I can bare the burdens of my soul, knowing our conversations are private and I am not judged falsely. I am directed with care and compassion towards healing. These women are true counselors as well as friends.

In addition to professional resources and wise friends and confidants, let me recommend a workbook that may be helpful for some of you: *When War Comes Home: Christ-Centered Healing for Wives of Combat Veterans*, by Chris Adsit, Rahnella Adsit, and Marshele Carter Waddell. This book is a "work" book. Assignments require responses from you the student. It offers many helpful ways for improving your healing environment and gives you ways to nurture yourself.

There are many books available for the seeking person. While I have found several sources that have been of great value to me in the writing of this book as well as in my personal life, I am listing two at this point (one listed above). Another such book is *Once a Warrior, Always a Warrior: Navigating the Transition from Combat to Home* by Charles W. Hoge.

After much advice to the warriors, Colonel Hoge makes a comment to spouses and family members that deserve our immediate attention: "It's not your job to change your warrior. They need to do this for themselves."[48]

We can only change ourselves. Therefore, we the spouses of combat warriors will benefit from protecting ourselves from becoming secondary victims. Most of Colonel Hoge's book is devoted to helping the wounded warrior, all of which is very insightful and user-friendly. One chapter is dedicated to spouses and for our purpose greatly increases the value of this book for our readers.

My first suggestion to all of us with struggling warriors—get help.

Archway—
Learn to Live

Years ago a song came out titled *I Hope You Dance* sung by Lee Ann Womack. While the title encapsulates the gist of the song, I suggest you listen to it often. I further suggest you live life now. Collect memories. The dishes left in the sink and the laundry filling the hamper will be there later, but memory-moments rarely come and tend to disappear quickly.

Several years ago, Charlie and I visited with Tony Haug who served as staff sergeant under Charlie in Vietnam. Later he became an officer and retired from the Army. Not far from his home on the west side of

Florida is a recreational parachuting grounds. Tony drove us there and encouraged us to take the dive. And we did. I don't think I had skydiving on my "bucket list," but when the moment came I grabbed it. I am so glad I did. My grandkids rave about the video of Grammy tandem-jumping from 13,500 feet. I have to admit it was a hoot.

Some of our finest family memories were camping trips. Several years we floated the Verde River in central Arizona. It could have been an easy day trip, but we stretched it into three days. The costs were minimal. The boats are gone and the boys have moved on to other things, but the memories remain priceless treasures.

My (Diana) parents died early in life. I was twenty-five when my mother, only forty-five, passed away. My father died thirteen years later. My memories of them are from my growing up days. The pictures captured in my mind are as invaluable as the photos in the family album.

The opening line to *I Hope You Dance* is "I hope you never lose your sense of wonder." I hope you never lose your sense of wonder either. The nicest thing about being alive and being a parent and a grandparent is wonderment. The world calls us to wander and wonder. Live life to its fullest. Life is meant to be explored and enjoyed.

And yes, we have all had our share of pain and disappointment. Our warriors are plagued with horrendous thoughts, memories, and nightmares. What greater reason can we give than to encourage ourselves to embrace our "dream" life and build new memories? Take pictures—the kind that stays in your brain, as well as the kind you put in frames and notebooks.

Live now! Got a dream? Follow it. Got a bucket list? Fill it to the brim.

Grief—a Brief Recap

Moving past grief to acceptance is like removing the gag order we wrap firmly around our hearts. The warrior risks humiliation, rejection, and abandonment. The wife may find herself rebuffed or in a twister being tossed like a boneless rag doll. None of these extremes resolves the innate problems associated with grief, but neither does an unnerving delayed move towards resolution. Understanding the cause of the warriors' grief has never been or ever will be a pleasant walk on the beach. However, it is a journey well worth the effort it takes to plan and proceed to a meaningful and fulfilling destination.

For those spouses of warriors who suffer from grief over lost Brothers and the loss of their innocence because of their experiences in Vietnam, be encouraged. Grief can motivate behavioral changes. Satisfactory resolutions are attainable.

We, the spouses of warriors, know that as the "keystone" it is the desire within our hearts to support the pieces of the arch that opens the pathway for healing. We recognize that as the keystone, the pressure lies upon us. The failures and successes are not our responsibility, but opening up possibilities for healing are ours to pursue and enjoy.

Love is not rude.
It does not look out for its own interests.
It does not easily become angry.
It does not keep track of others people's wrongs.
1 Corinthians 13:5

CHAPTER 8
FEAR

This and the following two chapters are closely bound together—<u>Fear</u>, <u>Faith</u> and <u>Forgiveness.</u>

Think of them as sisal, a tightly braided, three-ply rope which is strong and durable, but subject to fraying when the ends are not neatly tied together. While these three elements—fear, faith, and forgiveness—can be disassociated, when woven together, they become synergistic. The whole is stronger than the sum of its parts. Fear is all consuming, even crippling, if forgiveness is not present. How can one forgive unless they have faith that encourages forgiveness of self and others? Therefore, we may conclude that like the rope, our effectiveness lies in the strength of all three components working together.

In this chapter we will cover the first element of our sisal rope—fear. In the next two chapters, we will look more closely at the other two plies of our three braided rope—faith and forgiveness—and how they all fit together.

Of course, I felt fear...

Captain Kenneth J. Costich (Vietnam 1969; 1st/ 16th Infantry) said, "From a personal standpoint, it is difficult to overcome fear...it is easier to ignore it and hang on a few minutes longer. It is even more difficult to forgive, because it is almost impossible to forget. Combat actually causes a change in one's brain chemistry which is what makes a cure for PTSD difficult...we can only learn to fight and control the symptoms."

"Of course, I felt fear," said Charlie Taylor. "Every day, before every mission, but then I would think of the legions that had faced combat through the centuries. If they could do it, so could I."

"Fear was always present on every operation. Looking death in the eye daily was a very heavy load for any young person to endure,"[49] said Jim Johnson.

Fear is a howling, haunting wind in the dark of night. It's a tsunami of horror mangling your thoughts and robbing you of rest. It's "the unknown of what was hidden on the stream bank or behind a nippa palm branch or in any tree line."[50] (The tree line was often less than fifty meters from the landing zone.) Or perhaps it's what gnaws your gut while climbing the tunnel-riddled mountain or swimming across one of the Delta's endless rivers and canals. For sure, its genesis is the anxiety of looking death in the eye day after day in Vietnam.

Fear—The First Element of Our Rope

Webster's Dictionary defines fear as a feeling of anxiety and agitation caused by the presence or nearness of danger, evil, and pain. It is the respectful dread when in peril.[51]

Fear for our warriors falls into two general categories: 1) Fear associated with combat and living in a combat zone; and 2) Fear after the war and on the home front. Whether in base camp or in the field, fear hovered over the warrior waiting to be detonated. Such fears as that of ambush, being captured, losing control, being killed or wounded ruthlessly dogged every warrior every minute of the day and night.

Fear badgers the warrior whether he's trudging through leg-sucking mud, climbing a mountain, or sitting on his bunk. The warrior struggles with anxiety before, during, and after every battle. Fighting or the anticipation of fighting stretches beyond wartime and into the future. Closure never comes. Coping may provide a sense of normalcy, but fear and its offspring lingers forever in the psyche.

In Country—on the Battlefield

Fear for the warrior may be defined as camping on hell's front porch twenty-four hours a day seven days a week in enemy territory. For the Vietnam veteran fear was as close as his skin, night and day, for 365 days or as it was in some cases thirteen months or longer. Some warriors returned to Vietnam for another tour of duty. Fear was and is unrelenting, unmitigated suffering then and still today. Fear is slow to dissipate.

Among the many manifestations of fear are pestering, preying questions, personal questions, often so personal they cannot be spoken. One such question is, "Would they, the brave and honorable who served in combat, be perceived as weak simply because they feared for their life and the lives of friends when all hell exploded around them on the battlefield?"

One of Charlie Taylor's greatest fears had to do with his performance as a warrior and officer. He didn't want to be perceived as lacking. In fact, he would tell you that most men feared being labeled as a coward. Many performed heroic deeds, not because they were brave and felt like a hero, but because they were passionate about their duty towards their Brothers and, God help them, cowardice was not an acceptable option. The Brotherhood is a sacred trust. No Brother would be left behind, and no medic would leave a Brother unattended regardless of the risk to themselves.

Experts say, "It takes only a few moments of reflection for warriors to acknowledge that their greatest fear is not death but failure, and the shame that accompanies failure. More than anything else, warriors fear letting themselves down and letting their leaders and friends down at a moment when it matters most. They fear most not losing their lives, but their honor."[52]

Another fear common among the warriors was the fear of losing control of his emotions, his mental faculties, and behavior. Fear plagued the warrior during the war and continued to torment them when they first returned to the States. It may taunt them for many years after the war and most likely for the rest of their lives.

Quite understandable since on average the infantryman in Vietnam saw about 240 days of the 365 days he was in Vietnam in combat.[53] Lest someone think otherwise, the remaining days were not spent at the resort swimming pool. The combat warrior never escaped imperilment.

Charlie Taylor has said he could be asleep and distinguish the difference between incoming mortars and outgoing artillery. He could hear the "boob" of an incoming mortar round hitting the base of the tube.

In essence, the soldier never truly relaxed. Even in their sleep, they anticipated the next volley of bullets and mortars. Indeed, the combat warrior never had a moment's reprieve from danger. Base camps were inviting targets for the enemy. Sleep deprivation wreaks havoc with the nervous system and psyche. It was a no-win situation with long-term consequences both physically and emotionally.

For Terry Gander being in control is very important. He said, "I was scared the entire time I was in combat, and I never want to experience that kind of fear again. Now nothing scares me." And Donna, Terry's wife, replied, "I believe him."

Dr. Jim Johnson puts it this way; "The jumble of feelings that most of us experience changes from time to time, and the uncertainty of what we feel and why we feel it often causes us to fear that we might lose control. It's like being at the top of a waterfall, very close to the edge. At the bottom of the raging waters are the foam and rushing waters of rage, grief, fear, guilt, desperation, and the fear that we just might slip over the falls."[54]

Have I ever known such fear—fear that stalks you, plagues you? Yes and no. I've known fear, but like most of us, fear has been a passing horror. For the Vietnam combat veteran fear was daily—from sunrise to sunrise to sunrise. It didn't just go away after the warrior left the battlefield. The memory remains but a breath away. Such is so for Terry Balfe. Although he experienced many battle engagements, he tells of one encounter, he will never forget.

On February 26-27, 1968, Terry Balfe faced death. It was only by the grace of God that he survived to tell this story. "All day the battle raged. I got separated from my platoon when I went to rescue a friend of mine who had gotten shot. This was a buddy, a Brother. Of course, I went when he called for me. That evening I connected with another unit and was put with four other soldiers whom I didn't know out on a listening post. All hell broke loose about 3 A.M. Three of the four soldiers were killed within 20 seconds. I shot all my M16 ammo and all but one M79 round. The two of us who had survived thus far started to pull back. Then I was hit with four bullets on the right side of my body. The other soldier was shot once in the stomach. We found a small bunker that had been cleared that day. I pushed the other soldier into the bunker, and I crouched in the opening of it. About an hour or two later, we could hear the VC whispering. They were not more than three feet away. I fully expected to be captured or killed, but God answered our prayers and a helicopter gunship came, strafed our position, and saved our lives."

Stateside—After Nam

Barbe and Terry Balfe have been married over forty years. They sometimes speak about the events that took place in February of 1968, and the numerous other events of that year-long fear. Today, when the moment is right, they share what Terry's experiences were like more than forty years ago. Barbe said, "When we talk about the 26th and 27th, the real nitty-gritty of it is avoided because Terry is rarely in the mood to go there. But we have talked several times about his feelings of knowing he was going to die and what an unimaginable feeling it is. Just recently he remembered that after the panic and fear of acknowledging death was imminent, there was a sense of calm. At that point in our conversation he got up out of his chair flailing his hands saying, 'That's enough, that's enough' and even though his spirits were good, he felt he was getting much too close to that feeling again."

Ron Miriello recounts when he feared it would be his last day on earth. "Our boat was cruising at the maximum speed of eight mph and I was in my .50 caliber gun mount. Suddenly, we were under heavy small arms and rocket fire from the nearby jungle. I began firing rounds as fast as I could, scared shitless, watched a B-40 rocket land close to my mount, then a second one closer. I knew death was facing me in the eye if a third round continued to be zeroed in on me. Out of nowhere, an F-4 Phantom jet dropped a five-hundred-pound napalm bomb on the enemy positions. I felt the heat and it was one beautiful sight. I owe my life to that pilot."[55]

Debbie, wife of Ron Miriello, tells us that even today; "Ron is always aware of his surroundings, he closely observes behaviors of others—

unashamedly profiles people. He almost never sits with his back to others, likes to see everyone and everything in the room. He always sits where he can see all entrances and exits. Ron says he just can't stop this practice, and if he does, he feels very uncomfortable or anxious. If he cannot see all entrances when we are eating, he gets indigestion."

Many of the combat veterans we've come in contact with mirror Ron's behavior, a behavior mixture of fear and caution. We will revisit these responses more in a later chapter on hypervigilance. Hypervigilance is an inescapable behavior pattern drilled into the warrior during their military training and greatly embedded in their heads and muscles during combat. While from a spouse's point of view, vigilance can be a trifle annoying and on some occasions humorous, nevertheless, it is a lifesaving device that we as wives have learned to expect, respect, and appreciate. Heaven help us, we spouses should become more alert to our surroundings. It just may save us a great deal of pain or even our lives.

Fear—the Heightened Awareness of Danger

In eerie quietness the soldier feared the enemies' sudden burst of bullets. In the rustle of foliage and the crossing of countless waterways, the warrior and his Brothers felt exposed to VC attacks, a hidden booby trap, and a command-detonated bomb. In the din of battle, the warrior feared death, or worse—being captured. Fear had no mercy; it was unforgiving.

Whatever the basis of fear, it is not an enemy, but one of many emotions that may be confronted with reasonable expectations of success. For as surely as we breathe, fear unchecked wreaks havoc with the warrior's psyche and his youth. Fear may be the first alarm to danger, in which case it may save your life. For the warrior under combat fire fear may run amuck. It is a Venus flytrap devouring youthful naiveté. It makes young men old, and old men bitter.

Dr. James Johnson said it this way, "They came as boys and left as old men."[56]

Love does not rejoice in iniquity,
But rejoices in the truth .
1 Corinthians 13:6

CHAPTER 9
Faith—The Second Element of Our Rope

"O God, help me!

Dr. James Johnson said, "In the midst of an ambush when all hell has broken loose and one cannot think because the noise of explosions and gunfire is tearing one's nerve fibers to shreds, asking for God's help may be the only utterance one can make."[57]

He continued, "Ron Miriello avoids being seated in places where people are at his back. However, Ron said, 'God grants me complete comfort in His house even when seated in the front and this amazes me. My abilities to deal with my combat trauma are simply gifts from God. It is only through the grace of God that I remain strong emotionally.'"[58]

"And Dave Schoenian says, 'The Lord has guided me my whole life. We all have hardships, but you must have faith to get you through.'"[59]

Not all who find themselves in a foxhole facing death find God to be loving and merciful. Some doubt His presence. Perhaps the most frequently asked question about faith is this: Where is God when it hurts?

Guy P. Moore says, "The God I once knew died in the battle at Can Tho on February 26-27, 1968, when my company was wiped out except for twenty-six men. To this day I still have trouble getting close to God."[60]

I personally believe that God can help us withstand the upheaval caused by war. Twelve-step programs encourages its members to believe in a "Higher Being"—a being with power that exceeds the addict's own abilities. I believe we benefit from looking beyond ourselves for something or someone as our source of strength. Belief that a workable solution to a full and happy life beyond the grinding down of emotions we call fear is possible. For me, that belief is centered on God. The Bible says that love casts out fear (1 John 4:18), and God is the source of that love. I can't love as I should in my own strength, but with God's help I can love and stay the course.

Terry Gander expresses it best: "I'm unique in God's creation; He has made me as I am, as different from other people as the lion is from the lamb. In Christ all differences disappear and my love for others is increased, just like the lion and the lamb. We'll dwell in harmony and peace."[61]

If fear is an illegitimate child conceived in war, and I believe it is, then let faith and forgiveness be foster parents, thereby giving the warrior an opportunity to receive nurturing. Let faith bring unity where wholeness flows easily between the veteran, the family, and their faith in a healing and loving God.

But faith has another element—belief in oneself. For the wives of combat veterans, it requires faith in the innate goodness of our warriors. Asking and receiving forgiveness may be a giant step in the right direction. Our faith in a powerful, caring God may make the first step in the healing process easier.

Susan Tuzcu speaks eloquently regarding her spiritual journey. "When Erol and I first met I was "religious," we had many discussions about it. As I have aged, I've come to know the true living God for who He really is and not some figment of my imagination. Through all of our troubles I have grown closer to the Lord. I have learned to trust Him and realize that 'In *all* things He works for the good of those who love Him, who have been called according to His purpose' (Romans 8:28). First Thessalonians 5:18 says 'In everything give thanks; for this is the will of God in Christ Jesus for you.'

At the time I was not very thankful," she continued, "but as I look back I know that it all worked for good and I do thank Him. My faith was a mustard seed thirty-three years ago. It isn't even the largest of garden plants yet but He isn't finished with me yet. I also see a good work started in Erol and God has promised that He will carry it on to completion until the day of Christ Jesus. I know He who promised will do it."

Action – *The Tie That Binds Frayed Edges*

In *Once a Warrior—Always a Warrior*, Dr. Charles W. Hoge speaks of four skills that may help the warrior deal with stressful situations. The first and most important to our discussion is called "Resiliency Inoculation Training."[62]

Most of us understand the word *inoculation* because we have had bazillion injections "inoculating" us from all kinds of physical diseases. Dr. Hoge borrows two terms from the mental health profession to describe this "inoculation" process. They are "*habituation* and *desensitization*...which in this context mean growing accustomed to things that normally distress you or that you react strongly to."[63] He uses the word "habituation" and "desensitization" to mean getting used to annoyances to the point that you don't notice their existence. This requires you to place "yourself in everyday life situations that trigger your distress or avoidance reactions and to gradually increase the 'dose' until these situations don't cause the same degree of reaction."[64]

I went through a series of desensitization inoculations for airborne allergies. It worked, but I did it under the care and observation of a physician. I suspect the process recommended by Dr. Hoge may be equally successful. I strongly suggest you consider this process. For some who suffer from war-related fears, it may be beneficial, but maybe more so when done under the watchful eye and guidance of your counselor.

Hoge has given us a viable solution which for many warriors is a "can-do." Let us suggest a few actions for the "keystone" spouse that may be of help to both wife and warrior.

Pathways to Healing

Lord, make me an instrument of thy peace.
Where there is hatred let me sow love;
Where there is injury; pardon;
Where there is doubt; faith;

Where there is despair; hope;
Where there is darkness; light; and
Where there is sadness; joy.
O Divine Master,
Grant that I may not so much
Seek to be consoled as to console;
To be understood as to understand;
To be loved as to love;
For it is in giving that we receive;
It is in pardoning that we are pardoned;
And it is in dying that we are born to eternal life.
St. Francis of Assisi

Archway—
Make Peace with God

Terry Gander says, "There was a time in my life when I denied my faith due to the effects of my combat trauma. Anxiety and depression blocked my faith from aiding in my healing process. This lasted for years. Once I began to heal and partly control the effects of my trauma, I began to regain my faith in God. I began again to read the Bible. I read about the lion and the lamb, which gave me a peaceful feeling inside that I had not felt in years. I knew then that God was by my side to help quell the effects of my trauma."

Perhaps you share a similar experience. Allow me to summarize Howard Rutledge's story of survival in the Hanoi Hilton.

When Howard Rutledge's plane was shot down over Vietnam, he parachuted into a little village and was immediately attacked, stripped naked, and imprisoned. For the next seven years he endured brutal treatment. He was frequently cold, alone, and tortured. He was sometimes shackled in excruciating positions and left for days in his own waste with carnivorous insects boring through his oozing sores. How did he keep his sanity?

In his book, *In the Presence of Mine Enemies*, Rutledge gives a powerful testimony as to the importance of Scripture memory."

Rutledge said, "Now the sights and sounds and smells of death were all around me. My hunger for spiritual food soon outdid my hunger for a steak. Now I wanted to know about that part of me that will never die. Now I wanted to talk about God and Christ and the Church.

'Every day I planned to accomplish certain tasks. I woke early, did my physical exercises, cleaned up as best I could, then began a period of devotional prayer and meditation. I would pray, hum hymns silently, quote Scripture, and think about what the verse meant to me.

'All this talk of Scripture and hymns may seem boring to some, but it was the way we conquered our enemy and overcame the power of death around us.'[65]

Like most of you, neither Jim Johnson nor I (Diana) are strangers to heartache and pain. What we have found is that God does not remove us from the ugly, despicable realities of life, but he makes the journey easier because he is always with us. We find comfort in reading the scripture and praying. Beautiful hymns and choruses sooth the ruffled soul. It is our prayer that you too will find your strength and solace in God.

Archway—
Communicate

Communication is an art that can be learned and practiced. Start with honesty—not judgment, but thoughtful and caring truth. When you don't understand something, ask questions. Let your yes be yes, and your no be no. Practice encouragement. Find something good with which to compliment your mate. Seek to understand his dreams. Don't be a "fixer." We all know people who think they have all the answers and can fix anything or anybody. Enablers wear thin in short order. Dwell on the positive.

Good communicators ask questions, then they listen before and after giving advice. A good communicator may agree or disagree with your opinions and your choices, but will respect your decision. Poor communicators who don't care what you think or feel may just throw you over a cliff.

Communication is not just verbal. Body language plays an enormous role in our interactions. Body position can read as someone overbearing or someone to be trusted. Hand gestures and voice inflections may confirm or distract. Practice good skills, and learn how to improve your communications skills.

Sometimes communicating with a warrior requires no response, but a great deal of concentration. A listening ear may be perceived as unspoken compassion. And such may be exactly what the warrior needs. It may be all exactly what the "keystone" spouse needs as well.

Communication leads to community,

That is, to understanding,

Intimacy and mutual valuing.[66]

Rollo May

Love bears all things,
Believes all things,
Hopes all things,
Endures all things.
1 Corinthians 13:7

CHAPTER 10
Forgiveness

Having looked carefully at the first two strands (fear and faith) of our journey using the illustration of a three-ply sisal rope, let us now address the third strand—forgiveness. Fear debilitates, faith fortifies, and forgiveness sets us on a road of managed recovery. Woven together (fear, faith, and forgiveness), we have the synergistic effect that strengthens the rope and empowers us to move forward with our lives.

In a generic sense "forgiveness" means to pardon. In its expanded definition, it means to give up resentment against or the desire to punish; to stop being angry. Furthermore it carries with it the relinquishment of our claim to punish or extract penalty for an offense.[67] It leaves room for error and weakness. Simply said, we choose to overlook a wrong.

Forgiveness includes forgiving others and forgiving ourselves, and in some cases, it means asking for forgiveness. Never easy, but most often healing. Sometimes we forgive a wrong perpetrated against us. And sometimes, we are required to pardon ourselves for the wrongs we've committed intentionally or unintentionally. Forgiveness becomes extremely difficult where reconciliation is risky or impossible. However, holding a grudge and/or withholding forgiveness from self or others may have physical and emotional consequences.

Deeply embedded in my brain is an unkind, rash statement I once made to my mother. In fact, in my ignorance and arrogance I've made several very rude and selfish comments to my mother. One day I was especially insensitive. I was in my early twenties, and should have known better. To compound the issue and to my dismay, she died a few months later. I never had the privilege of asking for her forgiveness. Forty-four years have passed and given the opportunity, I would beg for her forgiveness. The best I can do is forgive myself, which is easier said than done.

In light of the combat veteran's experiences in war and his spouse's trauma since the war, my regrets seem a bit trivial, but I tell of it to make a point. Regrets are unmerciful. Only through true forgiveness can one break the stranglehold of self-loathing. Only the healing of memories can release the fettered soul of the combat veteran and the grief-bearing spouse.

In the previous chapter we stated that fear fell under two broad and general categories: 1) Fear associated with combat and living in a combat zone, and 2) Fear after the war and on the home front. We might propose at this point that forgiveness also falls into these two broad and general categories and to that add the emotional comments and observations of the spouses.

On The Battlefields

When I think of Vietnam, I think of the brave warriors who gave and received orders to serve their country under life and death situations—their mission assigned and confirmed under oath when they entered the military. I think of the complexity of their training and their obedience under fire. Some lived while others died. Young men soon became old under the pressures of war. Memories, good or bad, live in our hearts and heads forever. War poisoned the warrior's self-image and his moral code was obliterated. Brothers stood together then and continue to stand together. No one has been left behind physically or mentally.

On the other side of the world, the president and politicians determined the rules of engagement. I think of it as Ping-Pong politics—strike and retreat. The "Brass" stationed in Vietnam played chess with tactics using our men in the field as pawns. They were doing their job. Surely our embattled veterans have a right to be angry.

Not only does the grunt lose his youth and innocence, but the officers who fought beside them and played a critical part in the survival of these young men paid a high price for their participation.

Captain Kenneth Costich, who commanded C Company 1st of the 16th Infantry in Vietnam in 1969, said, "No matter what we did as leaders, some of our soldiers were going to die or at least be seriously maimed. I still second guess myself on virtually every order I ever gave in combat…there is no peace from that, there is only the hope that whatever orders I gave saved more men than they killed. The deaths of my men haunt me."

We easily understand why Captain Costich's memories haunt him. Under the same or similar circumstance, we too would feel incapable and perhaps undeserving of forgiving ourselves. Could this picture be further complicated? Yes.

On the Home Front for the Warrior

If the bludgeoning of war wasn't bad enough, our returning veterans came home only to face rejection by those who garnered their information and misinformation regarding the war and the warrior from a boisterous virulent few, primarily the press—a subject I address in chapter 2. Rules of engagement were determined by politicians—another topic covered in chapter 2. We bring this back to your attention to explain the "why" our warriors were angry and how we might build a logical foundation for forgiveness.

Dr. Jim Johnson said, "Coming back to the States, some of us were labeled as malingerers and having had personality disorders since childhood. The denial of our government tethered with the lack of understanding of those to whom we returned has made us all realize that there are no flak jackets or steel helmets for the soul and mind."[68]

Ray Shurling, a personal friend of Dr. Johnson and combat Brother who served with a Special Forces in Vietnam as an adviser to a Vietnamese unit, said, "Time and again I have asked God to forgive me. Maybe he has…but forgiving myself is another matter."[69]

Let me say, in summary, that the veteran has every right to be un-forgiving. He watched his Brothers die. Thousands of returning warriors were wounded. War poisons the warrior's self-image and his moral code is obliterated. The warrior was ridiculed and in some cases ostracized when he returned to the States. Yes, he may have trouble forgiving himself and others, but in not doing so, he may prolong healing emotionally and physically. Holding back forgiveness increases stress within the body and stress leads to illness, mentally and physically. It also may lead to heart disease and cancer. Sadly, stress may lead to major personal and family contentions as well. Not forgiving is destructive.

On the Home Front for the Spouse

Take a deep breath. Most of the women I have spoken with have talked about the rough times they have had in their marriages because of the trauma that their husbands have experienced. So, let us consider this: Do we need to forgive our warriors and those who "managed" and "mismanaged" the war?

Lynne Moseman says, "Roy, like most husbands, takes his anger out on the ones he loves the most. I don't do well in confrontations and have a hard time fighting back. I usually just cry and keep my thoughts to myself. This has caused both of us, along with our son, much grief through the years. Roy has a short fuse and yells first and eventually calms down. It's difficult at the time to constantly be the cheerleader in the family. I am always telling Roy not to be so negative. We are so blessed, it's hard to understand why he is always so down on everything and everyone. Honestly, I got tired of him taking everything out on me. He gets angry for no reason, hurting my feelings and then apologizing later and expecting everything to be all right.

"Our son has learned not to take everything his father says to heart. Many times I'll call our son to explain his father's behavior. I hate that PTSD has sometimes been a barrier between father and son."

Donna and Terry Gander were married after their children were adults. Terry's children had very little knowledge of Terry's Vietnam experiences—not a situation that Terry wanted, but such was the case. He thinks his boys feel that he was just "unsociable" and that he didn't care for them as much as their mother did. Donna said, "We are hoping that we can bridge that gap. So I gave them a copy of Dr. Johnson's book which includes Terry's involvement in the Vietnam War. It would do them all good to try to be on the same page and be able to talk freely about Nam and their past. My heart hurts for him," she adds.

JoAnn Moore said, "My career enables me to make friends and go places where Guy doesn't like to go. The only social activities we share are the military reunions."

Jim and June Carolus struggle to have an intimate relationship. She said, "He tends to be distant with me. He is afraid to get close—afraid he will lose me and get hurt again."

The trauma of losing Brothers in Vietnam has often overwhelmed Jim. Now he fears that if he loves June too much, something awful will happen to her, and he cannot face another loss. June longs for closeness.

Jim spent two tours with the Marines in Vietnam. On the second tour he kept everyone at arms' length. It was just too dangerous to make friends and then have them die. This stiff-armed relationship is not uncommon for the warrior, but it is very difficult for the family, especially for the spouse.

One wife told me that her husband is suicidal. His doctor keeps him as stable as she thinks any veteran with severe PTSD can be. Yet he withdraws into himself, leaving her to "make the most of it." Of course it makes her sad, angry too.

Susan Tuzcu said, "The predominant emotion I feel concerning the actual experience of [my husband's] trauma is profound sadness for what he endured and for the loss of his youth and innocence. I also feel the extreme pride and admiration for his bravery, endurance and ability to complete the tasks set before him. I am envious of the bond that he has with those with whom he served. The emotions I feel concerning the results of trauma or his behavior resulting from the trauma have been anger, bewilderment, and sadness."

Barbe Balfe, whose husband endangered her during his nightmare, says, "Think about the kids whose father nitpicked at everything they did or didn't do. Think about the parties we would like to have gone to, but our warriors couldn't stand being in a crowd. And what about those nightmares, the kind that become loud and violent?"

I remember being deserted while vacationing on a tropical island when Charlie had a flashback. I remember tears and many of you remember them too. We remember the withdrawals, the depression, and the rages. For some it's lack of trust, to the point of not wanting to fully commit to a loving relationship. Some remember days and years of self-medication. It hasn't been easy. It isn't over.

Can we forgive?

Forgiveness: What it is…and What It Is Not

Forgiveness requires change. When we acknowledge a wrong and realize the power it has over us, we have come to a crossroads. We can continue on the road we've been traveling or we can take an alternate route. If we continue in the direction from which we came, we can expect more of the same. If we choose to turn away from the past, we accept the opportunity to improve our status quo. Over and over again, experts say forgiveness benefits the one forgiving. We can choose to hold a grudge, point a finger, revel in our pain, or seek revenge, but to do so is crippling us, regardless if we are the offender or the offended. The choice is ours. Packaged with forgiveness it has the potential for personal rewards—peace, joy, relief to name a few.

Which brings us to another element of truth. Forgiveness is loving yourself. Let me once again refer to the Serenity Prayer which encourages us to accept that which we cannot change; to change what is possible to change, and to have the wisdom to know the difference. It goes on to stress the importance of living one day at a time and enjoying one moment at a time.

Most of us from the Vietnam era are approaching our seventh decade and some have embraced it full force and are moving into the next span of life. We are old enough to grasp the virtue of the Serenity Prayer. We have faced hardships and overcome most of them. We know that troubles shadow our future, but let us also remember that shadows come because somewhere there is light. And I believe that light comes from our efforts to forgive ourselves and others.

The power of this prayer lies in our willingness to forgive ourselves and others for those things that we cannot change. To do so is to love ourselves, to be kind to ourselves. When we love ourselves in a healthy manner, we are free to love others and thus forgive them.

Twin to the idea of forgiving ourselves is setting boundaries. Fortify your resolve to forgive by practicing forgiveness every single day for the big and small offenses and all things in between—daily. Every bridge has pillars that anchor it against the storms and the wear and tear of normal activities. Those pillars are reinforced so as to withstand forceful elements that might otherwise crush the bridge. Setting boundaries reinforces our bridge and helps us withstand the stress of today and tomorrow. Practicing or exercising those boundaries will further strengthen our ability to face the new and unexpected which we all know is inevitable.

One of the benefits of setting boundaries is that we get in touch with ourselves. In so doing, we become aware of our behavior patterns. We know what triggers anger and depression. And, in essence, boundaries become our choice. We take responsibility for our actions and feelings. We choose to not just survive but to bloom and grow. We test and try our instincts of what works for us individually. When those choices are crossed or offended, we become analytic. We get in touch with that which can be changed and thus we have an opportunity to become more flexible. As we become more flexible, we also find self-acceptance and tend to judge ourselves and others less severely.

In the book *Forgiveness: Heal your past and find the peace YOU deserve*, Lori S. Rubenstein gave a list of what she had learned from forgiving. Here are a few of those things: "I learned that forgiving

1. is not about me being stupid or being a fool;
2. is not about forgetting what happened;
3. is not a sign of weakness or neediness;
4. does not mean I must trust him again;
5. is not about my duty to punish someone for their behavior as though I was the Karma Guard, God, Judge, Jury and Prosecutor all at once;
6. does not mean I instantly feel at peace."[70]

Forgiveness: Why we should….

The quick and simple answer to why we should forgive is this—it promotes health and well-being.

Lack of forgiveness manifests itself within us both physiologically and psychologically. Bursts of anger and bouts of depression may often be the visual demonstration of unforgiveness. Lack of trust, feelings of guilt, and hope of revenge are some of the unseen aspects of the psychological trauma connected to an unforgiving spirit.

On the physiological side of things, an unforgiving attitude may precipitate heart problems. No doubt all of us at one time or another have experienced anxious moments and during those times, we've felt our heart rate and blood pressure accelerate. Rubenstein goes on to say that, "Numerous research projects have found that when you hold on to hurt, anger and bitterness, cortisol is continuously pumped into the body causing ill health, disease, and even cancer."[71]

In a report from Mayo Clinic entitled *"Forgiveness: Letting Go of Grudges and Bitterness,"* the author says, "By embracing forgiveness, you can also embrace peace, hope, gratitude and joy."[72] Forgiveness doesn't imply forgetting. It doesn't minimize or justify wrong actions. We can forgive without excusing the act. "Forgiveness can even lead to feelings of understanding, empathy, and compassion for the one who hurt you." Forgiveness is a commitment to a process of change."[73]

Terry Balfe, like many of the warriors, has some anger issues. Barbe said, "In the first thirty years of our marriage I did all I could to not be the cause of Terry's anger. Sometimes I could do nothing right and I mean nothing. Same with our kids, especially when it came to schoolwork. Terry sees that now and is very apologetic about it. In fact, he's come a long way. He has apologized to each of us and I have truly forgiven him and the past. I can't speak for the kids but it's obvious that they love him or they wouldn't want to be around him so much."

Barbara Bedell said, "My husband, Metz, fumes over the injustices precipitated by the war, but hides his anger often behind his humor."

Marianne says, "I understand how PTSD works—at least in my own husband's case. It doesn't make it any easier for either of us except in knowing that angry words spoken are not really meant to be the bullets of emotional pain that they are. As hard as it is for me to watch this and bear the brunt of the outbursts, I now realize that it is equally hard for my husband to go through it. I understand that just as he is pushing me away, it is a time when he needs me the most to help shore him up from his mental pain. He trusts me implicitly, and I him.

We both know that PTSD will always be with us. But knowing that, I would marry my husband again in a heartbeat."

That's forgiveness! Forgiveness lessens the offense and allows for healing of emotions and relationships. Forgiveness is about change—change for the better.

When we acknowledge a wrong and realize the power it has over us, we have come to a crossroads. We can continue on the road we've been traveling or we can take an alternate route. If we continue in the direction from which we came, we can expect more of the same. If we choose to turn away from the past, we accept the opportunity to improve our status quo. Over and over again, experts say forgiveness benefits the one forgiving. Packaged with forgiveness is the potential for personal rewards—peace, joy, relief to name a few.

Building and Rebuilding Bridges

Rifts between family and friends are painful. Whenever possible, repair the fences and add gates that allow healing and understanding. Nothing could be more compromising to our physical and psychological well-being than unresolved differences. We will explore more of this (i.e., anger and guilt) in the following chapters.

In his book *The Art of Forgiving: When you need to forgive and don't know how,* Lewis B. Smedes tells the Bible story of the Prodigal Son found in Luke 15. Allow me to summarize the story.

The son feeling restrained by his father, family, and the farm decided to see the world. He asked for his inheritance which the father gave to him. The son headed for "greener" pastures. After squandering his wealth on whims and wishes, the son finds himself hungry. He decided to return home, intending to become a servant in his father's household. The father expected his return and had fully prepared to forgive his son and return him to his position as "son."

What can we learn from this story? First, the father chose to overlook the offense. Second, the father did not demand revenge, although such was his right. Third, the father restored his son as a true son and member of the family.

Would that we could all follow suit—forgive ourselves and others and return to a state of wholeness. It is a spiritual and emotional journey that releases us from the burdens of our past, brings healing into our present, and garners joy for our future.

Like the earthly father in the story of the Prodigal Son, the heavenly Father awaits our return. He forgives our wrongs and restores us to health. He strengthens and blesses us so we can move forward. Relationships with friends and family are renewed. Our hearts and minds are restored. Hopes and dreams for a fulfilling future are ours for the taking.

Conclusion

Someone has said that healing a memory is like dying. Perhaps it is, but healing is possible and well worth the struggle. Dr. Glenn R. Schiraldi said, "Forgiving self means to give back to oneself the life that went before the trauma."[74] Is such a thing possible? Yes. When we forgive, we honor ourselves and honor the memory of our lost Brothers.

Love never fails.
But whether there are prophecies, they will fail;
Whether there are tongues, they will cease;
Whether there is knowledge, it will vanish away.
I Corinthians 13:8

CHAPTER 11
Become Friends with Your Warrior
...and Yourself

We know of no stronger friendship than that experienced in the Brotherhood of our warriors. Common history and common experiences transcend all barriers. Time has little effect on the importance of this bond. We are eternally grateful for the bond that ties our warriors together. It makes their journey in this troubled world bearable and meaningful. We cannot change the past, but we can influence the future.

Such a bond exists for the spouses and often for family members. It may not to the same extent, but it may become more so over time. As we spend time together and share our common struggles, we build our resolve to stay the course and become better, stronger, more productive persons.

Aristotle said, "In poverty and other misfortunes of life, true friends are a sure refuge." A true friend bears our burdens without judging our motives. Encouragement is strong medicine that can heal the soul and spirit and body. Samuel Goldwyn said, "When someone does something good, applaud! You will make two people happy."[75]

I have several very close women friends. These are women who listen and care, but it is Charlie to whom I cling. He is my very best friend. I would covet that same relationship for all wives. What is our key? Communication—open, unbridled conversation daily. Oh, dear ones, make your spouse your friend. I fully acknowledge this isn't always possible, but when it is, go for it.

A best friend makes you stretch and grow into the person you were meant to be. A best friend knows when to listen and when to advise. A best friend may agree or disagree with your opinions and your choices, and friends don't throw you over a cliff.

Here are four quotes to consider:

- "A man that hath friends must show himself friendly." (Proverbs 18:24)
- "A real friend is one who walks in when the rest of the world walks out." (Walter Winchell)
- "The only way to have a friend is to be one." (Ralph Waldo Emerson)
- "You can make more friends in two months by becoming interested in other people than you can in two years by trying to get other people interested in you." (Dale Carnegie)

Embrace Your Own Strength

"There is a fountain of youth: it is your mind, your talents, the creativity you bring to your life and the lives of people you love. When you learn to tap this source, you will truly have defeated age." (Sophia Loren).

Outside my living room window is a hummingbird feeder. Sometimes there are twenty or thirty birds flying about. The hummingbird is the only bird that flies backward and every other which way. They maximize their strength—their ability to fly. While they will perch, they don't hop across the grass. Their legs are small and weak. From that I deduce that we should maximize our strengths and minimize our weaknesses. Why not do the same for our spouses and ourselves?

Experiment with Incremental Adventure

Move away from your comfort zone, but in small increments. Find ways to help another warrior and their family. Go to school/college. Start a "bucket list."

Charlie had always wanted to be a paratrooper, but the jump school class he had been assigned to while serving at Ft. Lewis Army Post would deny us any time together before he shipped out to Vietnam. So he chose not to go. It is one of his regrets.

As mentioned earlier, a few years ago, we were visiting Tony Haug in Florida. Tony had served as a squad leader with Charlie in Vietnam. He later went on to OCS (Officers Candidate School), became an officer and made the Army his career.

Near Tony's home is a recreational jump facility. At Charlie's request, Tony took us to the airfield where Charlie spent the day learning how to jump solo (and land!). I decided to do a tandem jump. Late in the afternoon, we took the dive—from 13,500 feet in the air. We have pictures to prove it. It's been on Charlie's "bucket list" for a very long time. We are glad we took the opportunity for an awesome adventure.

As a rule, most of us are into less drama. We all have dreams, but if you don't, now is the time to start that bucket list. It may be reading a certain book or writing a poem. It may be to see the ocean or climb Pike's Peak.

Whatever your dream or bucket list—pursue it with passion. Years ago, I purchased a "Grandparents" calendar. Included in that was the story of an eighty-eight-year-old great grandmother who was training and competing in triathlons. My idea of exercise is to do it the first five minutes of the day and get it out of the way. Triathlon? Not for me. On the other hand I'm passionate about dreaming big and fulfilling those dreams. One dream right after the other. I encourage all our readers to dream big.

Take Back Your Happiness

Never underestimate the power of laughter. Happy people are optimistic. They are active and have healthy habits. All of the previous archways we have spoken about in this book are enhanced when we are happy. Happy people tend to absorb the bumps and roadblocks in life with a tad more resilience.

Ask yourself, "Is my cup half full or half empty?" If it's half full, you probably find joy and satisfaction in your daily routine. If you find your cup half empty, know that a change for the better is possible. Are we saying that happy people don't experience disappointment and stress? No, but what we have seen is that happy people don't coddle dejection day in and day out. They explore options and find solutions.

As a keystone in the archway, we spouses may find bringing happiness and most especially humor into our warrior's life a challenge, but one well worth the effort. Husbands don't come with an extension cord that you can plug into the electric current and they immediately light up and dance like some Christmas decoration. As a matter of fact, neither do we. Humor connects us with others and brightens our situation. Humor may be temporary, and joy can be cultivated and become innate.

Happiness is a mental and emotional state. It's having or showing a feeling of great pleasure and contentment. Synonyms include such things as joy, amusement, satisfaction, gratification, euphoria, and triumphs. We as Americans have been told that we have a right to pursue happiness. Yet we have found that happiness is not in possessions or in materialistic comforts. Mark Epstein said, "Happiness is the ability to receive the pleasant without grasping and the unpleasant without condemning."[76]

Let me (Diana) brag on my co-author, Dr. James Johnson. Jim struggles with PTSD and a number of physical ailments. Yet he continually reaches out to help others. In so doing, he has received countless notes, letters, emails, and face-to-face comments of gratitude from his readership. He is not grasping for fame and fortune. Neither is he railing on his misfortune. He is simply loving each of his Brothers. Regardless of the personal sacrifice, he is bringing a ray of sunshine into their dark world. Such does not bring laughter, but heartfelt satisfaction. Perhaps we could call it triumph. He is once again walking with us, guiding us (both warrior and wife). He shoulders our pain. Surely there is joy in knowing it was the right thing to do and he did it well.

As "keystone" wives, we long to lighten the warriors' burdens and our own. How can we do that? Let me suggest five ways.

- **Be courageous.** Barbara Cannode is an active member who in 2014 served as president of the Ladies Auxiliary of the Military of the Purple Heart. She continues to work to bring help for spouses of PTSD and TBI (Traumatic Brain Injury) veterans. June Carolus writes poetry, some of which is included in this book. She opens a window to the soul. Her work will encourage you to strive for the high road. Her message—you are not alone.

Barbara Bedell and her husband Metz are the cornerstone of the 5th/60th Infantry reunions. Metz's organizational skills and his computer savvy make our reunions run smoothly. He is a great example of a duck floating serenely on the surface, but paddling furiously beneath the visible water. Only the hotel staff and the reunion committee know how much diplomacy and skill it takes to make a reunion a success. Metz's attention to detail spells success for the attendees and guests.

- **Be a good listener.** Last year I had the privilege of meeting Pam Rogers. She and her sister, Donna Gander, are good listeners. They shook the community loose and brought about one-on-one support for veterans with community members. They listened to what Terry Gander (Donna's husband) had to say with their ears and their hearts. Marianne listens. She hears Bill's angry words and hears his emotional pain. In response, she wrote *Raven's Light~A Tale of Alaska's White Raven,* Publication Consultants, 2008, an allegorical story of a raven suffering from trauma due to the oil spill in Prince William Sound, Alaska near Valdez, Alaska. It teaches us to see PTSD for what it is and encourages us to be longsuffering. Hope sings center stage.

- **Be optimistic.** Fighting PTSD is a bit like an infant learning to walk. They get up, they fall, and they get up and try again. Sally C. said her husband was spit on and booed when he returned to the States. Together they have found a more promising life. Barbe and Terry Balfe have celebrated over forty wedding anniversaries. Celebrating their fiftieth in a few years rings with optimism.

- **Laugh.** Barbara and Metz Metzler have found humor to be the bridge over a canyon of horror. Like many other veterans, when someone asks Metz when he was in Vietnam, he might say "last night." But with all the troubling memories, he still maintains a warm smile and a terrific sense of humor. Dan and Mary Galde recently married off two of their sons. When you think of marrying off your military brats who are now in their forties and marrying within a month of each other, you have to have a few laughs. Laughter never saved a downed pilot, but laughter lightens the burdens life brings.

- **Dream, Organize, Implement**. I did not dream of writing this book, but I dreamed such a book would be available. I've organized and reorganized a dozen times, and little by little I'm implementing the dream. Charlie, my dear and patient husband, proofs and advises my work with caring, courteous comments. Dr. Johnson has encouraged, critiqued, and corrected this work. His suggestions for content are invaluable. I could not and would not have written it without his approval. Nor could I have gotten it finished without Dan Galde and the women who faithfully responded to my questions. The dream is only one element in the writing of this book. Those who have teamed with me to write this book hope and pray that the reading of it will help many. As "keystone" wives who want to bring healing and wholeness into their homes, I encourage you to dream big, organize well, and implement soon.

Whether or not you understand
The challenges facing you
Today or tomorrow,
Understand that God is working through it
To prepare you for what lies ahead.
Stand tall and face the winds of adversity.
Lance Wubbels

CHAPTER 12
DEPRESSION: Physical and Mental Needs

"When we were younger I didn't realize a lot of Terry's actions were signs of depression," said his wife Barbe Balfe. "I certainly do now. He told me awhile back and then again recently that he knows for sure that if he hadn't married me, he definitely wouldn't be here now. I remember a few years ago he was joking about how I would be better off without him, and I responded not only denying that to be true, but also most importantly, I told him, I'm planning on us being together after this life, and you better not ruin my plans. Furthermore, if I go first and am sitting there waiting for him, and he doesn't show up, I will go looking for him. I won't be happy about it either. All kidding aside, I think he got my point."

"I didn't do enough in the early days," Mary Galde admitted. "I don't think I knew enough about what was happening to Dan. Now, I constantly encourage him to get help, but I think he still feels he can handle it on his own. He takes medication for depression—and that's good—but it's not dealing with the real issues. Dan doesn't like to 'air his dirty laundry'—a favorite phrase of his. He's never been one to share many things with other people. So counseling is very hard for him."

Dan C. suffers from depression and has been suicidal at times. He has been hospitalized a number of times. His wife, Barbara, says that without his meds there is no sleep, and when he is in a deep state of depression, he can and will sleep 16 to 18 hours at a time.

Depression—An Oppressive Fog

Simply defined, depression is experiencing low spirits, gloominess, feelings of despair, and/or sadness. Loss of self-worth and confidence and withdrawal often accompany these emotions. For most, depression includes decreased functional activity, and in its worst state may lead to suicide. It has been said that twice as many Vietnam veterans have died by suicide since the war than died at the hands of the enemy.[77]

One of the first questions I asked myself is what is the genesis of depression? Is it anger? Guilt? Unrequited grief? The second question I asked was how does a spouse recognize the danger signs? My third question is what does the spouse do when all signs point to depression? And fourth, how does the spouse protect herself from becoming a victim?

First—Some Perspective on Combat

I doubt that any amount of training can prepare a warrior for the mental trauma of combat, even though the military does its best to train and equip brave men and women. The skills that are taught become so ingrained that the warrior's body responds as if it were created for such a purpose—aggression, hypervigilance, keen sight, and hearing. This is rightly so and absolutely necessary. A warrior must be alert and forthright. Never is it more necessary to be defensive than when you're winding your way through the jungle, fording rivers and canals, and climbing mountainous terrain anticipating the enemy anywhere, everywhere, at any time. It never quits. And then the warrior comes home and he's expected to turn his warrior button to the off position, but instead, it's stuck on replay. The result: The warrior becomes anxious, stressed, depressed, and maybe suicidal. Peace for his soul is as foreign as an ice pick in his eye.

The grunt, noncommissioned officers, and company grade infantry officers in Vietnam were constantly on search and destroy missions. They also were easy targets for any hidden away enemy. In fact, in most cases they were bait for the enemy. Why else would they drive up and down highway 4 in the night? Yes, perhaps it was to slow the enemy from planting bombs in the road. And why did they hop on a Huey at dawn day after day and pray they returned? Because the strategy to draw the enemy from hiding never ceased. The enemy and their supplies poured into the region like killer bees to a hive day and night, week in and week out.

There was no rest in the field. When the warrior closed his eyes at night, he cradled his weapon to his chest. The cover of darkness invited trouble, and it came carte blanche. Even back at base camp, with the first thump of a mortar hitting the base of the launch tube and the sound of an AK-47 peppering his position, the warrior in base camp rolled from his cot and headed for the bunker.

Andy Robertson served with the Third Platoon, Bravo 5/60th Infantry 9th Division and later with the 1/16th infantry battalion. When he arrived in the country February 6, 1968, the TET offensive was going strong. The smoke in Saigon drifted over the Delta region leaving an eerie omen and dread for the new troops. Andy was issued a weapon, but no ammunition. After his three-day "training" he and his comrades were sent out fully equipped for a bit of field experience. It's **February 10th**. About 2 AM, they had incoming small arms fire. After an hour, they marched full-out back to Bear Cat.[78]

"No matter who's shooting," Andy said, "there is no more terrifying sound in the world than the sound of bullets coming in your direction and popping over your head traveling 2500 feet per second. It wouldn't be long before we could tell the difference between the sounds of AKs (the enemy's weapon of choice) and the M16s (U.S. military weapon) firing and the difference between merely close and deadly close."

The chronicles below, used with his permission, cover the first two weeks of Andy's experience in Vietnam. These are but a few snippets from his journal. His yearlong experience reflects a sampling of what the war was like for most combat veterans.

February 12th, Andy and his buddy, Kenny, were flown out to join B Company, 5th Mechanized Battalion, 60th Infantry, a company that had suffered about 75 percent casualties in the last twelve days (days! not months). B Company would have six company commanders in less than two months.

February 13th, Andy is sent 300 yards outside the wire on a three-man listening post. He said, "I was scared shitless, mostly because I had no idea what we were supposed to be doing. I didn't sleep for a minute all night. The base camp got mortared and we were radioed to come in about 4 AM."

February 14th, Charlie Company was ambushed out on the highway and their company commander, Captain Donald Dick was medevaced. And so it went on **February 15th** and again on the **16th**, and then again on the **17th**. These nighttime ambushes went on throughout the next week.

February 16th, another Company is ambushed at 2 AM. **February 17**, the second platoon spotted 100 VC at 11 PM moving in. They called in artillery and reinforcements. **February 18th**, "Across Vietnam, the communists hit 45 cities, district capitals and military installations with heavy rocket and mortar attacks.[79]

And so it went—day after day, night after night, week after week, and month after month. If a warrior was lucky, he came home at the end of the year, but the war never stopped. The replay button refuses to budge and the sounds and horrors of war continue to echo in the minds and hearts of our warriors. Is it any wonder that our veterans are depressed—one of several serious symptoms of post-traumatic stress disorder? It's enough to make anyone depressed.

As I read Andy's account, I am struck by the unrelenting demand for battle readiness, and I know from speaking with him and other combat veterans that the emotional and psychological impact was horrendous. Dr. James Johnson's book *Combat Trauma: A Personal Look at Long-Term Consequences* often speaks of the frustration, the disgust, anger, grief, and other strangulating emotions. And like malignant cancer cells, they grew and grew until they threatened life itself.

Speak with any one of the wives and friends who have participated in the writing of this book and they will tell you that the hellishness experienced by their warriors hasn't missed a day to exercise its brutality since the day their veteran returned home—forty-plus years with little or no relief. Depressed? I guess! Depression might be compressed and managed, but it floats to the surface and pollutes the shoreline constantly and randomly. It is ever present.

We, Charlie and Diana Taylor, recently watched the Hollywood version of the battle for Hamburger Hill. Even this horrific battle cannot be fictionalized kindly. But I'm not here to discuss the merits of our heroic men who scaled this mountain. Neither am I going to attempt to assign demerits to the stupidity that followed when the military did not move in and maintain ownership of this strategic military height—albeit I would love to add my opinion more strongly. What I do want to bring out is a common phrase used over and over in the movie—one that my warrior-husband assures me was a typical response to unresolved emotions. It was a way of accepting status quo. Simply said, but with deep roots that would later bear much grief and depression—"it don't mean nothing."

"It don't mean nothing?"

Nothing could be farther from the truth.

Jim Carolus tends to be distant from his wife, June. He is afraid to get close to her because he is afraid he will lose her and be hurt again. He stays within himself. He has to work at not being depressed and he does say the memories of comrades lost in battle sneak in periodically. He takes antidepressants and meds at night so he does not have nightmares.

In his book on combat trauma, Dr. Johnson said, "Losing comrades through death or injury and to never see them again does mean something. What can be disabling is 'the persistent sadness some of us experience that results from the strong memories of combat, guilt, and unresolved grief over the loss of our Brothers and even from the 'loss of innocence' that many of us experienced with the first gunshots from the enemy.'[80]

Erol Tuzcu continues to have raging periods of sadness when he recalls an event of February 20, 1969, in Kien Hoa Province. A/3/60th flew on what was thought to be a routine mission. As the helicopters dropped the troops, the landing zone proved to be very hot as the enemy opened up from several sides.

"Erol says, 'The feel, sights, and smells and the horror that occurred after we landed was to be with me the rest of my life. Several 105mm rounds had been rigged as booby traps and each time one would explode, several Brothers would be hit. My buddy Mirick was walking point and tripped one of the rounds, blowing off both of his legs. I applied tourniquets and continued to dodge bullets but Mirick bled to death with me lying next to him with absolutely nothing I could do to save him.'"[81]

Susan Tuzcu, Erol's wife says, "I believe Erol has suffered from depression probably since I have known him. He is not debilitated by it, but I feel there is always a black cloud."

"It don't mean nothing?!"

On the contrary—it's like very powerful C-4 plastic explosive in a Claymore mine ready to explode with little provocation and often at an unsuspecting moment. If you don't die from the explosion, I assure you, the fragments will do great damage. Pent up depression is as deadly as a claymore.

Depression can be unrequited grief. The warrior never had time to grieve for a lost comrade. Neither did he have time to assimilate the loss of his boyhood innocence. Such grief often manifests in dark depression and moving into the light seems hopeless. Depression is a lot like finding yourself in an ocean of despair, without a life vest, miles from the shoreline, and with no hope of rescue.

Terry Gander grieves for some Brothers he left behind in Nam. He feels guilty for being able to come home to his family, when many others could not. Such grief is shared by most combat veterans. So it does mean something. We strive for what is worth our struggle—the man, our warrior, his hope for happiness in a chaotic world.

In *Achilles in Vietnam: Combat Trauma and the Undoing of Character* the author, Jonathan Shay, M.D. Ph.D., says depression in the combat veteran is seven times more likely to occur than within the age-similar populous. Combat veterans are "eleven times more likely to have suffered from dysthymic disorder, a chronic, fluctuating state of depression, hopelessness, loss of self-respect, and loss of energy for living."[82] The concept of a healthy marriage is illusive and suicide is common.[83]

Such need not be the case for most. There is hope and help. Don't misunderstand. All men sustain loss in the throes of battle—the loss of personal innocence, the loss of comrades, and the greatest of losses—peace of mind. War slices and dices the heart and soul, the core of a man. Healing may be possible but visible scars are inevitable.

"I had no desire to live any longer," said Guy P. Moore.[84] But JoAnn, Guy's wife, had other ideas. After twenty-nine years of marriage, JoAnn knew her husband pretty well. She begged him to please give inpatient treatment a chance. Guy did not think he could learn how to live a better and happier life, but he was soon proven very wrong.

"Out of desperation, I entered the North Chicago VA Medical Center combat trauma unit for five weeks, and I can truly say, that these five weeks were the most productive weeks of my entire life."[85]

There is hope. There is help.

Buried somewhere in the recesses of our warriors' memories are those who have died, who had they lived might well be our friends, neighbors, and family, but they died in that awful war.

Memories branded on the veterans' brain shackle their souls. Let us strive to break the fetters of depression which may be in part a battle to forgive—forgive ourselves for a past that cannot be rewritten or forgotten, forgive the government for what they have said and left unsaid, forgive society for the pervasiveness of lies which have added salt to the emotional open wounds.

Depression—the Masked Bandit

I must say that I approach this topic with a sense of trepidation and urgency—trepidation because it rings of fragility and urgency because lives and futures are at stake. Depression is common among those with PTSD and thus deserves serious study. Why do I call depression the "Masked Bandit"? Because under the mask are the real problems—issuances that can be dismantled and dealt with one by one.

Along with the definition on page 115 of this chapter, depression can also be defined as a decrease in functional activity or an emotional condition, either neurotic or psychotic, characterized by feelings of hopelessness and inadequacy. I may incorporate feelings of diminished self-esteem, hopelessness, shame, and pessimism. It is a treatable condition, but may require in-hospital therapy and, in some cases, medication.

Drs. Laurie B. Slone and Matthew J. Friedman in their book *After the War Zone* list the following ideas for coping with depressive symptoms:[86]

- Communicate with a close friend or family member about how you are feeling.
- Plan fun and enjoyment into each day.
- Be active. Exercise
- Break tasks into manageable, doable segments.
- Permit yourself to have feelings—bite size if and when necessary.
- Make time your ally, not your enemy.
- Eat healthy, balanced meals.
- Relax—quiet, soothing music may be just the thing.

Sometimes simple, methodical attention to one's lifestyle can make a difference for the person suffering from depression. Sometimes the depressed person needs professional help. Such was the case for Dr. James Johnson.

Jim said, "Just prior to my having to cease work, my sadness began oozing out, often via tears at seemingly unprovoked times. This greatly worried me and, at times, was embarrassing to me. For over three decades, I had held it together, never daring to allow others to see the stored-up sadness I was experiencing inside.

"While I was not clinically depressed per se, my frequent down moods were of increasing concern to me, especially with my being a therapist. Fortunately, I finally had the good sense to bury my pride and denial, and I sought help via the VA."[87]

Barbara Johnson, Jim's wife, said, "Withdrawal and depression seem to go together. Sometimes Jim is just not there."

Signs of Depression

Warning signs of depression include crying with no explanation, low energy levels, sleep disorders, and the inability to derive pleasure for those things or activities once enjoyed by the sufferer. A preoccupation with talking or writing about death, dying, and suicide are serious warning signs and should be taken seriously. Consumption of alcoholic beverages and drug use exacerbate the danger of suicide. In such cases, it is advisable that the sufferer gets professional help as soon as possible.

Simply said, depression is not just a feeling, but "a complex blend of thoughts, behaviors, emotions, and physiological changes that work together to keep a person 'stuck' in a dark mood."[88] Those who are caregivers to combat veterans can attest to the truth of this definition. And let us not underestimate the secondary effect that caregivers may become susceptible to. We too may begin to lose interest in activities that we used to enjoy and may also have sleep issues. We may begin to think there are no solutions and begin to feel helpless and—when it reaches the extreme—hopelessness. Here are a few suggestions that may help the spouse and the warrior manage the downside and hopefully bring positive, uplifting change for the sufferer.

Archway—T-I-M-E

Time is a precious and finite commodity and, in many cases, a gift. From feelings of hopelessness and helplessness to wholeness and productiveness takes time and energy. Embrace time as a close and caring friend. Life is not a sprint or a high-hurdle race; it is an adventure, an exploration. Hold a steady course. We hope and pray you will find a lot of compassion and a few miracles along your journey. We have used "time" as an acronym for the remaining four "Archways" because everything we do involves time. Let us grab it by the lapel and make it work for us.

Create Dreams
"T" – Text and Context
Manageable, attainable dreams. Believe in yourself.

Harriet Tubman said, "Every great dream begins with a dreamer. Always remember, you have within you the strength, the patience, and the passion to reach for the stars to change the world."

In "T"—Text and Context—Create Dreams, we look at the power of dreaming big dreams and the value of setting incremental goals to achieve those dreams. Always remember that we never go beyond our wildest dreams. So, dream big! In the above text, we shared from Andy Robertson's journal. And while those days were horrific, they are worth remembering because they built strong backbones and character. They are documented, defining events. Charlie Taylor, my husband, says, "I will go to my grave with the thought that leading men in combat was the most significant thing I have ever done."

Although a fine line separates "goals" from "dreams," we need both. To my way of thinking, setting goals speaks of scholastic, physical, or financial achievements. It is a well-known fact that written goals are more apt to become reality. The striving for business and personal success are worthy endeavors economically, physically, and psychologically. However, when I think of dreams, I think about something emotionally gratifying—the pot of gold at the end of the rainbow. Realizing a dream steps beyond the achieving of a goal. Together the pursuit of goals and dreams spike the joy of the journey and strengthens our inner core. The guts to pursue and attain goals and dreams lie within our hearts. Whether we are talking about goals or dreams, the roads to accomplishment are similar.

A worthy goal might be learning to cook; the dream may be becoming a gourmet chef. Physical exercise could become the first stage of getting in shape but the dream is a jaunt down the Grand Canyon or to climb all of the mountains in Colorado over the14,000 foot level. Have a dream? Then set incremental, achievable goals that ultimately lead to the fulfillment of your dream.

I encourage all of you to consider keeping a journal of your activities, lessons learned, and emotional fortresses scaled. In a few months' time it will become a road map. You will see your journey for what it is. If you need to make corrections, you will know what direction is needed or if some thing or event has been noteworthy, the written message will be worth revisiting. Know when and why you give yourself a pat on the back. Time plays an integral part in the realization of our dreams.

Walls or Bridges
I—Imagine That!

See yourself in a positive environment. In "I"—Imagine That! we examine the power of self-talk. What we say to ourselves about ourselves becomes the GPS guide for our behavior. The old adage for computer programming couldn't be more insightful—garbage in/garbage out. When it comes to programming the mental image we have of ourselves, how we see ourselves could become self-fulfilling prophecy. Make "time" your ally not your taskmaster.

Never underestimate the life-altering effect of positive self-talk. When Charlie, my shy husband, first opened his own business, he would begin his day saying, "I feel good. I feel happy. I just know something good is going to happen to me today." The energy generated by his comments changed his apprehensions to enterprise. Self-talk builds bridges to success and tears down walls barring forward progress.

Strive to eliminate "I can't" and "it's too difficult" from your thoughts and verbiage and as much as possible replace it with "I can" and "I'll try." Positive self-talk will reduce stress and enhance your enjoyment of life. According to a Mayo Clinic Newsletter some health benefits that positive thinking may provide include:

- Increased life span
- Lower rates of depression
- Lower levels of distress
- Greater resistance to the common cold
- Better psychological and physical well-being
- Reduced risk of death from cardiovascular disease
- Better coping skills during hardships and times of stress.[89]

Take Action
M—Mix/Mingle/Master

A few years back I came across this statement by the late Maya Angelou in the *DailyNews*, "Life loves to be taken by the lapel and told, 'I'm with you kid. Let's go.'"

We couldn't agree more. Make something good happen—mix, mingle, and master some activity that influences someone else in a positive way. Take action. Life presents a plethora of opportunity.

Service to mankind within the community and around the world creates a venue for removing the lethargy of our own problems into vital and rewarding solutions for someone else who may have needs we can uniquely meet. Yes, it takes time, but the Vietnam warrior may well be retired or may be approaching retirement. It is not time to build sandcastles and memorialize our own issues; it is time to help your combat Brothers, or the neighbor, or the child suffering with leukemia, or go on a mission trip with your church.

Inactivity is one of the drawbacks of depression. Incremental activity changes—one baby step after another—brings success into one's journey. Stop, look, and listen first at your own life, second at your community, and third at the global community. What has been achieved? What needs strengthening? What change might bring greater and more dynamic achievements into focus? We suggest you connect your personal action inventory to an important date, like your birthday or the New Year. We suspect it will become easier to mix and mingle when we see progress in our own lives and the lives of others.

In "M—Mix/Mingle/Master" we explore the plethora of opportunities in our communities for volunteer work. Here are several more:

1. Dresses for Africa – www.littledressesforafrica.org. *Mature Living* magazine recently had an article about "pillowcase dress ministry" and included the instructions. I recently became acquainted with Hope4Women International, a group headquartered in Tempe, Arizona, that distributes dresses for www.dressagirlaroundtheworld.com.

2. Kids Against Hunger is a nonprofit organization that packages a very specialized, highly nutritional soup mix and distributes it to orphans and others who are living in poverty.

3. For those who are feeling spry, check out Team Rubicon at www.teamrubiconusa.org. This organization began with a response from Jake Wood, a Marine who served in one of our more recent wars, and William McNulty, also a veteran. *The American Legion Magazine*, October 2012,[90] has an article on their work that is well worth reading.

I've listed several groups with a global emphasis whose activities range from the energetic to the more sedate. Most communities are inundated with needs and lack sufficient help. Our hope is that you will take action. The reward for your efforts will be worth your time and energy.

Calvin Coolidge stated, "We can't do everything at once, but, by God, we can do something at once!"[91] The future begins now. Grasp it and become a person of action and when you do, you will find that others will follow.

Read

E – Evaluate/Expect/Expectations

A wise man learns by the mistakes of others, a fool by his own.

(Latin proverb)

There is power in the written word. We have only to look at the effect *The Communist Manifesto* written by Karl Marx and published in 1848 has had on the world to appreciate the muscle of the press. Marx's work played a key instrument in the adoption of the socialist agenda. And let's face it: The U.S. would not have fought the Vietnam War if communism hadn't been a threat to the freedom we enjoy as citizens of the West.

In comparison, think of the Bible, a book that has topped the best-seller lists for decades. Many lives have been turned 180 degrees simply by reading and believing in God, His love, and His provision for eternity. Thousands of books, poems, and songs have been written claiming the power of God and His Word. Many of our laws and much of the U.S. Constitution are based on the Mosaic laws written in the Bible. It strengthened the backbone of America's early settlers.

Beside these influential books are hundreds more. I recently read Andy Andrews' *Mastering the Seven Decisions that Determine Personal Success*. The book is phenomenal—a true guide to making informed decisions. One of the seven decisions is the "Guided Decision." Mr. Andrews said, "Wisdom in the words of successful men and women throughout history can be found in books. You are who you spend time with, and you are what you read."[92] I concur.

History and biographies top my preferences, and I highly

recommend they become a part of your reading habits. Learning from others' experiences can be relaxing and informative. They also give perspective on the ups and downs we experience in this life. Reading won't change the sheets on our beds or wash the pile of dishes that accumulate in our sinks, but it will chase the shadows from our humdrum existence. There is more power in the written word than you can ever imagine.

Nothing becomes more energizing than realizing that the past does not have to rule the present. Most biographies portray a progressive journey in someone's life over time and through tough times. Having learned something from these successes and failures, consider this three-step process for building a more positive future for yourself: 1) *Evaluate* your present situation; 2) Cast aside that which doesn't meet your *expectations* and cling to that which does; 3) Step forward and *expect* great things for your future.

We are fully cognizant that we live in a world where electronics rule. It has been said that our populace reads one book a year. I prefer books, but I have a thirty-minute stretch of open road on my journey into town, time I use to listen to CDs, fiction, and nonfiction. We strongly encourage you do something with long-reaching, positive consequences. By all means reach for that which is exceptional.

We also recognize that many have become slaves to entertainment. While we all need some relaxation, it is dangerous to be consumed with the pursuit of fun and frills. Yes, relaxation is essential to both our physical and mental well-being, but like all good things, when it is taken to extremes, laziness can potentially add to your lack of self-worth and become an avenue to depression. Production and gratification go hand in hand.

From the Experts

"The World Health Organization recently said that more than 350 million people suffer from depression globally. 'It is not a disease of developed countries, it is a global phenomenon. It's present in both genders and in rich and poor populations,' Dr. Shekhar Saxena, head of the WHO's mental health and substance abuse department, told reporters in Geneva."[93]

Depression is an aberration from normal behavior and one of several serious signals of PTSD. According to the fourth edition of the *Diagnostic and Statistical Manual of Mental Disorders (DSM-IV-TR)*, the psychologist's diagnostic manual: "the sufferer has experienced depressed moods for the major part of every day for nearly two weeks. It alters and disrupts one's mood, one's thoughts, one's body, and one's behavior."[94]

One of the most helpful workbooks we found on the topic of overcoming depression was written by Michael E. Addis and Christopher R. Martell titled *Overcoming Depression One Step at a Time: The New Behavioral Activation Approach to Getting Your Life Back*. If you or a loved one is suffering from depression, seek professional help and/or get this book, read it, and follow its suggestions. A chapter is allocated to each of the seven steps with clear instructions on how to implement them into your life. Allow me to state them:

Step 1: Identify situations and behaviors that depress you.

Step 2: Find alternative behaviors.

Step 3: Select alternative behaviors and schedule them into your week.

Step 4: Adopt an experimental attitude.

Step 5: Try out the new behaviors and observe their effects.

Step 6: Evaluate the results of the experiment.

Step 7: Continue trying new experiments.[95]

Several of the spouses of our team members have needed and received help from professional counselors. Life is precious and a gift that should be enjoyed. When you need a guide to see you through the dark and lonely moments of depression, please get it. Don't put it off. Do it now.

"Many years passed in Ella and my relationship before I went to the Vet Center to start my process to try and choose life, instead of death," said Dave Schoenian. "I wanted to keep my family, not destroy the ones that meant so much to me. I never realized what I put my family through all those years, nor did I care at all. My wife said to me one day, 'I'm tired of being in the Goddamn army, every frickin day. Will it ever stop?' I can't help being who and what I am. Always the platoon sergeant," said Dave. He got help.

At the beginning of this chapter we quoted Keith Armstrong as saying that depression was not just a feeling, but "a complex blend of thoughts, behaviors, emotions, and physiological changes that work together to keep a person 'stuck' in a dark mood."[96] Those who are caregivers to combat veterans can attest to the truth of this definition. Our hearts are grieved by the pain so many of our combat veterans have experienced. Let us join our hands, hearts, and prayers to bring healing to the Band of Brothers. There is hope and help. Please do yourself and your loved ones a favor and reach out for help. You deserve to be whole and happy.

Below is a letter from Pam Rogers. Pam is Donna Gander's (Terry Gander) sister, an independent consultant project manager, and corporate advocate in the healthcare industry. She embodies many of the key attributes of a friend, companion, and soul-mate.

A Message of Hope
A Letter from Pam Rogers*

Greetings to All!

I had to think about this for a while, not knowing if I had anything that would be helpful to share. I guess the "I just gotta say it" in me prevailed...for I feel the need to briefly touch on this.

Depression...as we all know, takes on many shapes/forms (often denial for the warrior), compounded by PTSD which takes it to a whole new level. My observation is a reflection of my past personal losses and my most recent experience with this group. War in general creates havoc for the human soul, and all of those whom it touches. While a warrior may have in fact survived the war...the real fight began when they had to re-enter civilization, start processing all the suppressed horror, and attempt to put their shattered hearts and souls back together. I envision this literally as a heart/soul in a million little pieces in the midst of a reverse magnetic field, with the warrior groping for the scattered pieces. Surely, there are missing pieces and gaping holes in all of us.

I believe, the brain and heart of a warrior are tasked to overcompensate in order to deal with these unspeakable experiences. I realize that we cannot even begin to understand the bowels of hell they have already been through, and still…the battle continues for them every single day, to simply "cope."

Depression is a period of hopelessness and defeat, but we as God's children were put on this earth to be loving/nurturing life forces for each other. He puts us in places and surrounds us with people where we are tasked to become worthy of Him…which means we must continue to embrace our warriors and their families, trying hard to understand to the best of our ability the lessons we are to have learned from this experience.

I believe the newcomers to the reunion each year helps validate the real value of the continued efforts of our warriors to share/conquer/heal the demons buried within. They are each unique in their own experiences, and it clearly shows they still have a lot to offer each other—even if they don't believe it themselves. There are still many lost warriors out there, and it is my prayer that they too will eventually make their way to this circle of friends, a gleaming beacon of hope. I understand that unless one has walked in the shoes of a Warrior, we cannot grasp that true level of pain and suffering…nor can we deny HIS work in progress, for each of us…never give up, it is never hopeless.

Lastly, it means a lot to me to have been invited into this circle of friends, and I believe it is a healing journey for us all. Thank you for listening and for the continued sharing.

Many blessings,
Pam[97]

We leave you with this thought

If you have a pulse, you have a purpose. And when you pursue your purpose and persevere, anything is possible. Your potential is unlimited.[98] (Diana Taylor)

Life is 10 percent what we make it
and 90 percent how you take it
Irving Berlin

CHAPTER 13
Anger
"Anger is one letter short of danger."[99]
(Rajendra Tela Nirantar)

Guy P. Moore says he could easily write a book on his historical anger and rage. "They have cost me dearly since Vietnam. I have been in jail many times for destruction of property and fighting when I lost control. I have taken out my anger on numerous innocent people."[100]

Roy Moseman returned from Vietnam a much angrier person. "I was mad at the world sometimes and mad at everyone for no apparent reason," he said:

I am mad at myself even. I doubted myself for some of the things that I did in Vietnam. Some of the movies are so full of shit that it's a joke. I really get mad when I see how they portray the Vietnam soldier. I am sure there were some idiots in Nam who would do about anything just like there is in any society, but I believe there were very few who would intentionally kill innocent civilians and children. It just didn't happen the way Hollywood wants the public to believe. We were not a bunch of drunken, pot-smoking idiots running around in the jungle killing people. I hate the people that live in this country enjoying their freedom but protest everything they think of. At work, my biggest problem always was my outbreaks of anger. I would take things for so long and then I would explode. I would tell my boss what I thought of him and walk out the door. I would not take any verbal abuse. This is the main reason I opened my own company.[101]

Lynne Moseman said, "Roy, like most husbands, takes his anger out on the ones he loves most. I usually cry and keep my thoughts to myself. This has caused both of us, along with our son, much grief through the years."

Somewhere between the innocent young men who entered the military with patriotic thoughts and the grizzled combat veteran are two wars—the physical war fought in Vietnam and the emotional war fought within the core of their being. Somehow over time the physical war and the emotional war flip-flopped—the land known as Vietnam consumed the minds and hearts of the warrior, and the family and home became the physical battlefield. The wounded are not bleeding and dying on foreign soil, but emotionally and relationally in the dwellings we call our homes.

ANGER: The Common Emotion

Anger in and of itself is a common emotion. A little bit of anger may save your life; however, sustained or repressed anger may make your life miserable and can lead to illness and death. When our warriors engaged in battle, anger pumped adrenaline through the body. Their response to danger heightened their countercharge. The same holds true for all of us. When we are upset or angry, our adrenaline surges which causes us to be more alert and leads to a fight-or-flight response. A constant dose of adrenal hormones causes toxic physical changes that harm the gentle balance our body needs to be healthy.

According to Webster's Dictionary, anger is "a strong feeling of displeasure. In its variant forms, rage, wrath, and fury, it may result in loss of control causing injury and mistreatment. Rage takes anger to the next level. It is violent anger in action or speech, and is forceful and uncontrolled. Wrath implies usually righteous rage with a desire to avenge or punish.

In *Once a Warrior Always a Warrior*, Dr. Charles Hoge says, "Anger is a natural response to being threatened and an antidote to sleep deprivation and exhaustion; it helps to get the job done, and serves a vital function of offsetting fear. Anger and detachment are two of the most common emotional reactions that warriors experience after coming home."[102]

"In combat, anger was very common," states Dr. James D. Johnson. "The infantry soldier is trained to react quickly and usually anger was an asset in combat setting. When anger erupts, adrenaline and other chemicals enter the bloodstream, our heart beats faster, blood flows more quickly to the body, and muscles tense and strengthen."[103]

Guy P. Moore agrees. "I carried around a combat attitude and would react without thinking instead of rationally responding," he said. "That is exactly what I was trained to do in the army. I had no time to think through what was happening, only to react and usually violently."[104]

Barbara Cannode, wife of Dan, admits that; "Our eldest daughter is forty-one and very bitter towards Dan and me. I guess we did not have the perfect life she thought we should have. But please understand, we have three daughters and all three love their dad. It's just the coping that we all struggle with."

When asked what her emotions might be toward Dan Galde's trauma, Mary Galde said, "I guess helplessness is the most accurate description. There was no way I could remove the horror from his memory. It was a merry-go-round of hopelessness that eventually ended our marriage."

In his book *Deadly Emotions,* Dr. Don Colbert says that stuffed emotions have negative outcomes too. For instance, people who stuff their childhood emotions may become perfectionists. Some will deny failure and brush off criticism as it is not their problem, but their accusers'. Others will seek to control everything and everyone in sight. Still others who have low self-worth will engage in self-deprecation that manifests itself in self-doubt. They have problems making decisions or setting specific goals. Some become cynical and others become promiscuous in their search for acceptance.

According to Dr. Colbert, those who stuff their emotions are more apt to have powerful explosive emotions at a later time. "Emotions that become trapped inside a person seek resolution and expression. That's part of the nature of emotions—they are meant to be felt and expressed. Those who have stuffed negative emotions, especially anger and hostility for years, don't need much to set them off."[105]

What makes a warrior angry? Stupid! They don't do "stupid." Sending troops and ATCs (armored troop carriers) on "shooting gallery" missions down Highway 4 in the Mekong Delta at night infuriated Tony Normand. He called it "Road Runner" operations— "All we did was to be moving targets in the night for the VC to target practice."[106]

Charlie Taylor said, "My men hated being played like pawns in a game of chess when the top commanders began distributing men and arms as they thought best even though they were miles from the battle. War strategy may be learned from historical texts and may in some cases be useful, but those present on the battlefield faced life-and-death decisions and in most cases understood and acted on the here and now."

Being on the battlefield was the warrior's first war; coming home was his second. An acquaintance of mine (Diana), who had just returned from Vietnam, was accused of being a baby killer by his seatmate on a commercial flight to his hometown. Name calling was common. Some were spit on. Insults were rabid and uncouth. Vietnam veterans were often treated like lepers.

"Not having work clothes, Bob Nichols began working at his civilian job wearing his fatigues (without patches). One of his supervisors was an E-6 in the reserves and made a nasty comment that he was an E-6 and Bob only made it to E-5. Bob immediately reacted in anger and told him where he could put his stripes—that 'I got mine in combat.'"[107]

Some things never change. "Dissing" and hazing have filtered through societies throughout history. But one thing has changed and not for the better. Throughout the centuries people have been taught to live by the Golden Rule. It is time to reemphasize respectful behavior toward others. If we treat others as we wish to be treated, the world would be a better place to live and our schools and workplaces would be more productive and harmonious.

History bears out that Vietnam was a political war, but our virulent society hammered the warrior for their sacrificial service to the military. For sure, such things angered the warrior and, in most cases, those of us who had connections to our servicemen and women. It took years, but I for one am grateful to the Veterans Administration which has acknowledged and addressed our veterans' psychological and physical needs. Today's veterans have benefited from the persistent demands for recognition of the Vietnam War and the special needs of combat warriors. Their relentless struggles profited all military personnel. Have we reached perfection? No, but we have made positive inroads to better treatments.

ANGER: The Problem

Dr. W. Doyle Gentry gradates anger from episodic anger to chronic rage. He notes that "episodic rage," "chronic anger," and "chronic rage" are toxic emotions. People who experience episodic rage will be fine unless they are aroused, then watch out. Those who experience chronic anger may rant and rave, but do not reach a level of uncontrollable rage. The frequency is, however, unhealthy. Chronic rage is the worst-case scenario. It is dangerous and volatile.[108]

The consequences of anger are many. Anger causes fatigue. Anger affects blood pressure and places one at risk for a heart attack or stroke. Anger exacerbates high cholesterol. "Anger doesn't cause you to have high cholesterol, which places you at risk for heart disease. That basically comes from your family history. But there is no question that anger aggravates the problem."[109]

Chronic anger has the potential to generate chronic pain. Dr. John Sarno, professor of clinical rehabilitative medicine at New York University School of Medicine said, "Painful back spasms and chronic back pain often resulted from chronic tension, stress, frustrations, anxiety, repressed anger, and worry. Tension caused the blood vessels supplying the back muscles and nerves to constrict, thus reducing the blood supply and oxygen to the tissues."[110] When the blood vessels are constricted, they are unable to properly expel toxic metabolic waste from the muscles. In *Deadly Emotions,* Don Colbert, M.D., concludes that, "The result may lead to a diagnosis of fibromyalgia, fibrositis, myofascitis, repetitive stress injury, and other conditions."[111] He concludes that physical pain may be the result of unresolved emotional trauma.

Anger robs you of energy and can make you sick. It can also affect your career. It has been noted that those more likely to be injured on the job were angry, and the "angrier they were at the time, the more likely they were to be injured." In fact the chances of injury are five times more likely to occur when irritation is at the root of it. And injury is twelve times more likely where rage is an issue.[112]

ANGER: Managing Your Anger

Dan Galde faced life-threatening danger on every rescue mission he undertook in Vietnam. Some forty years later he vividly recalls searching for a downed pilot whose plane had disappeared in the dark depths of a river. The density of the darkness was both eerie and terrifying.

Mary Galde said, "When I look back, I realize that all I could do was hug Dan and try to comfort him. I felt amazing compassion, and was so proud of and amazed at his bravery. Now that I'm older and so many years have passed since then, I am full of regret that the military didn't insist that every warrior receive counseling to help them process the horror and cope with it."

Many of our veterans were not getting help. As I've said earlier, our Veterans Administration has made great strides in rectifying the problems associated with veterans suffering from Post Traumatic Stress Disorder. It has recognized the need for counseling and expended much effort into meeting this need, but the response has been slow in coming. Vet Centers also provide resources that help reduce the symptoms to manageable levels.

Anger is only one symptom of PTSD. Learning to manage this emotion may begin with participating in crisis and stress management programs. Educating oneself about PTSD and accepting appropriate help is the first step in a journey to wellness.

Another managing tool may be through self-knowledge. Know your limits. Seek ways to build your tolerance. That may mean you walk away from an explosive environment. Most of us want to have the last word. However, most arguments are not going to resolve the issues and, in most cases, they only create a greater division of opinions.

In his book entitled *Anger Management for Dummies*, W. Doyle Gentry, PhD, said, "There are many parallels between anger management and pain management."[113] He made several suggestions which are summarized below:

1. Find a quiet setting where you can be alone—a sanctuary where no one can interrupt. Give yourself at least ten minutes to savor an imaginary haven. Taking a "time out" is one of the simplest ways to manage anger. Grant yourself time and permission to cool down and refocus. Accord what time you need and get a positive perspective.

2. Rate your level of anger on a scale of 1 to 10 (10 being extremely angry).

3. Close your eyes and visualize peacefulness. For me (Diana) that might be relaxing on a sandy beach at the ocean listening to the pounding waves on the shoreline. There is something about the consistency of the sound and rhythm of the waves that soothes my anxiety.

4. Envelop yourself in the moment.

5. Recalculate your level of anger. If your anger level remains on the high side, repeat the process as needed. And don't forget that practice will improve your skill level.

Anger is often a festering sore. The more you ruminate, the more you stimulate your emotional response. Change unproductive, negative thoughts to pragmatic and creative opportunities. Talk to your counselor, a clinically trained chaplain/pastor, or a physician about your memories, those triggers that ignite uncontrollable emotions. Your future and well-being are well worth the effort. You are valued. There is hope.

ANGER: Perspective and Hope

In *Combat Trauma: A Personal Look at Long-Term Consequences*, Dr. James D. Johnson said, "Anger is like a fire, and our hurt or fear is like the fuel source of the fire. Unfortunately, stimulation of our hurt or fear can almost instantaneously produce the flame seen as anger. Our continual struggle is to experience our hurt/fear (anger) in appropriate ways, without hurting others or ourselves. This struggle is a lifetime endeavor for most of us."[114]

Wherein lies hope and perspective? For many it began at home with an understanding and tolerant wife. Barbara Johnson stood by Jim without questioning him even when night after night he rose from their bed and escaped to his office to journal his pain on tablet after tablet for many years. In like manner, Terry Balfe has been steadied by his devoted wife, Barbe. Terry Gander has found solace with his wife, Donna, and with Donna's family. Barbara and Dan Cannode struggled, but have stayed the course. Charlie and I have been blessed through the good and bad times.

Like Jim, Terry Gander found that "keeping a ledger" enabled him to manage his anger instead of it managing him. Jim's journals were later turned into books from which we have all profited.

Many warriors seek refuge in God. Dave Schoenian says, "The Lord has guided me my whole life. I have not done right by attending church much, but for some reason God has helped me and my family.

"Ron Miriello avoids being seated in places where people are at his back. However, in church, God grants him complete comfort in His house even when seated in the front and this amazes me," says James Johnson. Ron said, "My abilities to deal with my combat trauma are simply gifts from God. It is only through the grace of God that I remain strong emotionally."[115]

Guy P. Moore, Frank Martinolich, Bob Stumph, and Jim Johnson have all found help at inpatient treatment centers like Batavia, New York, VA Medical Center. Countless warriors have been helped through the services of counselors whether in private practice or through the VA Administration and at Vet Centers. Many also have valued from the guidance, encouragement, and support from other veterans and from military reunions, most especially from reunions of those with whom they served in Vietnam. Those who reach for help, find hope.

Having spent time looking at anger and coping methods from the warriors' perspective, let us now look at coping strategies for the spouses of warriors. I (Diana) think of them as "archways"—doorways placed strategically in walls that control the entrance to pathways to places near and far. The keystone at the top of the arch supports this "doorway." The spouse of a warrior, like the keystone, sustains and guards the future well-being of a household.

Let us now look at ways to improve ourselves, our outlook on life and the future, and strengthen our marriages and families.

Archway One—Encouragement

In *Encouragement Changes Everything*, John C. Maxwell says, "People go farther than they thought they could when someone else thinks they can."[116] All of us need a pat on the back from time to time. We crave encouragement. Therefore, let us be generous with giving encouragement and gracious when receiving encouragement.

I wonder where I would be without the bevy of friends surrounding and upholding me with encouragement. For me that involves occasional breakfast or lunch dates, phone calls, emails, cards, and a lot of prayer—just about anything that involves communication. I also suggest service clubs or benevolent organizations like "Big Sisters." The New Testament tells us that "it is better to give than receive" (Acts 20:35). Those who encourage and help others succeed, experience personal value and success.

Archway Two—Perseverance

Find your pathway through the trauma and press forward. Biblical commentary tells us that suffering produces perseverance, perseverance develops character, and character builds hope (see Romans 5:3-4). God help us! We all need hope in the midst of our suffering.

The dictionary defines perseverance as a course of action, in spite of difficulties, obstacles, or discouragement. When a farmer used a mule to plow his fields, he often put blinders on the mule so the animal would keep his concentration on the straight furrow and not be distracted from objects around him. For us as humans, perseverance means putting on the blinders and plowing forward. Sometimes living with someone who has PTSD, especially anger issues connected with PTSD, takes perseverance. We plod through the muck of life. The reasons we persevere may be many or few, but primarily we do it because giving up is not part of our makeup. Giving up means hopelessness and something within us innately lassos unto hope and hangs on. Hope dwells within our character. Hope envisions something better, and so we persevere.

Archway Three—Envision

In *Stress is a Choice*, David Zerfoss says, "For time and the world do not stand still. Change is the law of life. And those who look only to the past or the present are certain to miss the future."[117]

Call it your "Bucket List" or call it your "Book of Dreams." Dream big and fuel it for action. Six things come to bear:

1. Write it down.
2. Research it.
3. Find the time and money to do it.
4. Do it.
5. Journal your experience with pictures and comments.
6. Revisit your memories when you're feeling low and when you are feeling on top.

If something didn't come out like you had hoped, don't repeat it; learn from it. If it was successful and especially healing, relive it and repeat it. Good memories are penicillin to the soul.

Let's pray we never lose the ability to dream big dreams and envision ways of making them reality. Some would say that setting goals is more concrete than dreaming, but I think that anything we can dream about can become a reality, and we accomplish that by setting incremental goals. I dare say that much of our electronic gadgets were first envisioned and then incrementally designed—often with trial and error methods.

Archway Four—Goal Setting

Someone has said that if you aim at nothing, you are sure to hit it. So true. Let's talk about goal setting, a task that logically follows envisioning. Goal setting is a way of corralling a dream.

First we have to decide what we want. This is called the dream stage. This first step also includes envisioning the completion, seeing the beginning and the ending. Second, those who most often succeed do so because they write down what they want to accomplish. Some will at this point set a deadline.

I've followed those instructions as I wrote this book, but because of unexpected events, I've bumped the deadline several times. That's okay. Inflexibility, whether we are talking about time or the finished product, may give you ulcers. When I first started this book, I wrote a table of contents. Likewise, when you start a project, start with a list of small steps that can be accomplished in a reasonable time frame. Develop momentum and move consistently day after day. We all age one day at a time. In such a manner, we achieve goals one step at a time.

In *Stress is a Choice: 10 Rules to Simplify Your life*, David Zerfoss says, "The way you get meaning into your life is to devote yourself to loving others, devote yourself to your community around you, and devote yourself to creating something that gives you purpose and meaning."[118]

Archway Five—Humor
"Laughter is an instant vacation."[119]
Milton Berle

Nurture your sense of humor. Wise King Solomon said, "A merry heart doeth good like a medicine."[120] The Greeks sent those who needed healing to the "home of comedians." In medieval times kings and noblemen hired jesters to entertain their court followers. Most people today have fond memories of the Marx Brothers films, "The Three Stooges," and "Candid Camera" videos. Today's comedians add levity to our lives. Humankind loves to laugh and always has.

Humor promotes good physical and emotional health. Dr. James Walsh, author of *Laughter and Health*, wrote that there seems no doubt that heart laughter stimulates practically all the large organs…and heightens resistive vitality against disease."[121]

Studies show that rage and anger top the list of toxic emotions and generate an extreme stress reaction.[122] Allen Klein says humor doesn't replace our pain, but it does expand and lighten our burdens. Thus said, we can conclude that while humor may not supplant anger, it will dilute the effect it has on our physical and mental well-being. If you are the spouse of an angry person, laughter may not come easy, but it may bring a touch of sunshine into your existence.

Norman Vincent Peale said, "Our happiness depends on the habit of mind we cultivate. So practice happy thinking every day. Cultivate the merry heart, develop the happiness habit, and life will become a continual feast."[123]

Conclusion

Beware! A little bit of anger may save your life, but sustained anger will kill you. Anger can be dangerous, destructive, and deceptive. For the sake of your physical and psychological well-being and those of your loved ones, learn to master your anger. No one says it is easy, but all would agree that it is beneficial. If you find yourself holding onto or nurturing your anger, get professional help. If you are the victim of someone out of control, protect yourself. Seek counsel and stay the course. And by all means keep the faith in yourself and your abilities to make a difference in your life and in the lives of others.

THE WINDS OF FATE
Ella Wheeler Wilcox

One ship drives east and another drives west
With the selfsame winds that blow.
'Tis the set of the sails
And not the gales
Which tells us the way to go.

Like the winds of the sea are the ways of fate,
As we voyage along through life:
'Tis the set of a soul
That decides its goal
And not the calm or the strife.

What we know now is not complete.
What we prophesy now is not perfect.
1 Corinthians 13:9

CHAPTER 14
Flashbacks and Triggers

During our vacation in Bora Bora, Tahiti, Charlie and I biked three or four miles from the resort to a less-crowded, pristine beach to collect shells. We laughed and frolicked on the shore and in the surf. We had a wonderful experience, until suddenly without warning or explanation, Charlie jumped on his bike and peddled away leaving me to find my way back to the cottage. I was both stunned and peeved. I later quizzed him about his actions, but he was noncommunicative. So I set aside my angst. Much later that week, Charlie explained. "We were hit in Vietnam just at dusk. When the sun struck the tops of the palm trees, I had a flashback. I knew that any moment the shelling would rain down on us. I had to move to safe ground. It was as real that day as it had been forty-plus years ago." It took hours for him to calm down after the telling. I can only imagine his anxiety.

While touring in the southern part of China, we saw many people in black pajamas wearing conical-shaped hats walking the dikes of the rice paddies. Charlie spent the rest of the day sitting on the floor of the bus. These visual and painful reminders triggered unpleasant reminiscence of his combat experience in Vietnam.

Susan Tuzcu said, "Erol's triggers are kind of unusual and sometimes humorous. We may joke about them, but they are real and troublesome. One that is not funny is when the shower backs up with him having to stand in the water while showering. That drives him up the wall. When Erol was in Vietnam, he was constantly in water: stream crossing, water in rice paddies, and often having to sleep while lying in water. Almost always, if there was a firefight, one had to be prone in water while trying to stay alive during those horrible fights. It took Erol years to realize that when he was standing in water in the shower, it subconsciously took him back to those awful months in combat."

"But," she added, "My husband is an amazing man and I always thought he had nerves of steel. In 1979 he and I honeymooned in San Francisco. This man who had not been back from Vietnam that long took me on a helicopter ride over San Francisco. It wasn't until years later I realized how disturbing that was for him."

Triggers might be a spark that brings to mind anything connected to the original trauma—emotional, sensory, and physical reactions. Triggers may overload the mind and may explode into an unpleasant flashback. In flashbacks, the warrior feels he is reliving a past traumatic experience and it is just as real in the present as it was in the past.

Years ago Charlie and I traveled to Mexico. When we got off the plane, the smell of diesel and rotting jungle overwhelmed Charlie's sensory system. Thoughts of Vietnam destroyed any hope of having a pleasant vacation. The smells triggered a negative response much like what had happened when Charlie and I were on the bus in China. On the other hand, when dusk hit the tops of the palm trees while collecting shells in Tahiti, he had a full-blown flashback.

Flashbacks are like nightmares, except they occur while awake. They may be a fleeting moment or two, but the impact may last for extended periods of time. "The flashback usually involved an episode of combat, such as being wounded, seeing others wounded, sniper fire, fire-flights, major battles, preparing to go on a combat operation, being trapped and unable to move, and so on."[124]

"Roy Moseman has a small river that flows through his backyard. Sometimes he will be outside by the river and a UH1D (Huey) helicopter from the nearby National Guard unit will fly over. Roy said, 'No matter what I am doing, I sometimes feel that I am back in Nam and I am very aware of the chopper and I start watching the tree line on the other side of the river. I catch myself moving behind a tree for cover.'"[125]

Lynne Moseman, Roy's wife, said, "We were at a party with high school friends when Roy started to get upset and very emotional for no apparent reason. He said he thought he would start crying and not be able to stop. This scared me, and I wanted to go home but he pushed through it, and we stayed. I had no idea what the problem was."

Dr. James Johnson writes candidly about a flashback he had while in the hospital recovering from relatively minor surgery. Two days after the operation, he unknowingly injured his shoulder trying to lift himself from a bedside chair. It wasn't until the next morning he realized the full extent of this injury. He could not move and could not call the nurse for help. He began to sweat. His breathing became rapid and shallow, and his heart rate jumped. He realized these were the exact same circumstances he had experienced on March 1, 1968, with Company A, 3/60th Infantry when they got hit. He was blown into an empty canal and severely damaged his right shoulder. Now, thirty-eight years later, his emotions were again exploding. He lay helpless in the hospital bed sobbing uncontrollably...with an injured shoulder... and he had the same emotions he had four decades ago.

Barbe Balfe tells of her most frightening and potentially dangerous moment. "During the middle of the night I felt Terry moving onto his belly and getting up onto his hands and knees ever-so-slowly, as if in slow motion. I softly asked him what was the matter. He reached over me and grabbed the rifle that he insists must be loaded and aimed it at me. Somehow I stayed calm and whispered softly, 'Terry what are you doing?' Luckily, and at the same time, I was able to turn on the lamp next to the bed. I can still see the crazed look in his eyes. I've never seen it again, even in his rages. He pointed the damn gun in my face. I could feel the electricity from the end of the barrel as it wavered in front of my nose. I knew Terry wasn't looking at me. So I softly spoke to him repeating over and over that it was me, Barbe. 'I'm Barbe.' With that he lowered the gun, leaned back over me, put the gun down and went back to sleep—snoring at that. I calmly turned out the light and waited a few minutes. Then I woke him up."

Barbe said, "It was the scariest thing that has happened and this particular event occurred just a few months into their marriage." She cannot tell the story without becoming tearful.

Mary Galde said, "Dan didn't talk much unless he had been drinking. Then I found my reaction wasn't to his pain but to his drinking. I shed my share of tears, but I learned to be resilient. However, as I got older, it wasn't as easy, but in my younger years, I had to be tough. After he returned from the war, when he would have flashbacks—which happened with me a few times—I would stop and be concerned. Dan would brush it off, so the concern didn't last long. I remember when he came home from R&R (Rest and Recuperation) after the helicopter crash. His hands were all broken out in blisters, which is what happens to him when he's stressed."

Mary admits she has a strange ability to remove herself from painful situations. "Perhaps," she said, "it's from a lifetime of living with alcoholic parents."

Life is a schoolroom where we learn to contend with reality—good, bad, or indifferent. Mary learned to cope with alcoholic behavioral issues early in life. She had to be tough, even more so when it came to living with a combat veteran who turned to alcohol as a solution for his PTSD. Mary showed her mettle throughout the fray of her complex childhood and throughout many years of her marriage to Dan.

Donna Gander says she and Terry are closer now that they have learned to communicate more openly and more often about his war experiences. Donna said, "I feel free to ask him if he is having a bad day and why? He will usually tell me what's bothering him, but there are times that he does not. Possibly it could be a date of an event that happened in Nam or he is just reminiscing about a mission. I know now that his day-to-day emotions, his ups and downs, will be with him/us forever."

Flashbacks! –physical, emotional, and incapacitating—moments when the warrior feels trapped with the same feelings that occurred in the midst of heated combat. We cannot expect our warriors to pretend *it* didn't happen. Neither should we ignore our response to these fire-breathing dragons that leap unannounced into our homes and activities.

Flashbacks and Triggers—What are they?

A simple definition of a flashback is that it is a very unexpected memory of a horrific event that flashes into one's consciousness. Triggers are the catalysts that sparks a flashback.

Archways – Choices

Susan Tuzcu said, "When we were first dating he took the kids and me to a Fourth of July fireworks display. After we were married he refused to go ever again and that was when I learned how disturbing that was for him. Every Fourth of July and New Years when the fireworks are going off, he always tells me how much he hates it. He goes to bed early those nights. He will not watch a movie about Vietnam. One night we watched a World War II movie and I asked him why it didn't bother him. His response was, 'It wasn't my war.'"

When it comes to what happens to us, sometimes the choices are of our own making and other times they are not. Like Erol and Susan, Barbara and Daniel Cannode, and many of you, Charlie and I choose not to go to firework displays during the July 4th celebrations of our country's birthday. Fourth of July celebrations in Prescott, Arizona, are exceptional. They define all that is wonderful about our little town with its wild and frolicsome cowboy culture, and that which glorifies our nation. It is my favorite holiday. We love the parades and the rodeo, but we choose to avoid the fireworks display. Much to our dismay recently we had an auto accident. The incident and Charlie's response were not of our choosing. Charlie was traumatized, and during such stressful situations, he doesn't function well. We were 100 miles from home and scheduled to be at a family function. We opted to return home, but, unfortunately, not everyone understood our need for quiet seclusion.

Well, let's face it, sometimes friends and family members just don't get it and, to a minor degree, that happened in this case. I thank God we were able to work through the issues, but as many of you know, that doesn't always happen. Some people either minimize or exacerbate the stressful event. That brings me to this key question--what choices can we make to create equilibrium when trauma and drama collide?

Choice 1—Control

We can't control others. Most often we cannot control what happens to us, but given some space and time, we can choose to control ourselves and our responses to comments and events foisted upon us in our waking moments.

Daffodils will bloom and flourish even if buried in snow and even when night temperatures drop below freezing. Plant a daffodil bulb when the ground is warm and manageable. In due time, it will sprout and bloom. We can strive to build resilience into our lives. Taking that first step to master our response to negativity may take time and practice, but the results are worth the effort. Plant within your heart and head a plan, nurture that idea, and eventually, when the time is right, it will bloom.

Or to put it another way, think of living life like that of driving a car. First, we determine our destination. Then we sit in the driver's seat, place our hands on the steering wheel, start the engine, and steer down the road. Not everyone knows how to drive a car and very few know how to drive a semi, but driving improves with practice (most of the time).

I have not watched a lot of car races, but when I have and when there has been an accident, I'm amazed when the driver walks away seemingly unscathed. I'm equally amazed at the warriors who have suffered greatly from their gruesome experience on the battlefield yet who have persevered through life. I commend them for bravery in the field and throughout their lives as civilians.

Flashbacks, triggered by a plethora of who knows what, are to be expected. When they happen, the warrior may not feel he is in control of his responses. That's where we as spouses must step into the gap. I recognize that historically, most spouses have done so. When our warriors need help, we encourage them to get it. When they need a loving touch, we are there to give it. When they need and want to talk, we want to be there to listen. A kind word or deed makes a huge difference.

Ups and downs happen, but how we respond can be managed. When the ground is soft and easily cultivated, we plant and regardless of what adversity comes, buds eventually bloom. Life comes one day at a time. Let us welcome it. Start by determining the destination. Then let us put our hands on the steering wheel and start our engines. Let's take control.

Choice 2—Make a Difference

Let us weigh our options, pick the most viable for our situation, and make a difference. First, ask: what are my options?

In the example above, we chose to be in control and not to drift. Now let us think about choosing to be better and not bitter. Ask any warrior and he will tell you war is hell. The Vietnam War was over forty years ago, and we've had multiple wars before and after. Even when we win a war, the warrior is wounded. The trauma our warriors experienced in combat are indelibly inscribed on their brains. Not a one of us can change that, but we can choose not to be bitter. "Better" and war are not synonymous; however, there are good reasons to refuse to let that experience poison our hearts and freeze our forward movements. And that reason is "us." We are unique and life is precious.

One way to make a difference is to serve others. If our warrior is a member of the Military Order of the Purple Heart (MOPH), they can volunteer at the Veterans Administration centers—the Veterans Affairs Volunteer Service (VAVS). The VAVS handbook is available at the MOPH website. The Ladies Auxiliary also has VAVS.

If the idea of working with veterans doesn't do anything for you, find another avenue to serve. Most not-for-profit organizations have a need for volunteers. The local Catholic Charities and AARP have a need for someone who can help people do their tax returns. Many libraries have a program to help those who cannot read—adults and/ or children. The need is great. Meeting that need can be a great boost to all parties—the needy individual, the organization requesting help, and us, the ones fulfilling that need. Being a servant may not make us rich or famous, but it will enrich our lives and someone else's. When we pour a healing balm on someone's wound, we spill some on ourselves.

Coalition for Compassion and Justice (CCJ), a nonprofit organization in Prescott, Arizona, feeds and clothes many destitute people. They serve twenty-one meals a week, many going to the struggling, often homeless, veterans in this mountainous community.

Choice 3—Lay Stepping Stone

In 1995, I was diagnosed with non-Hodgkin's lymphoma. I know what it is to hear that dreaded word—cancer. I know what it is like to undergo treatment. Therefore, when I reach out to other cancer patients, I share in their experience. I can encourage them, because I know how they feel. Laying stepping stones is a bit like volunteering except more specific. As wives of suffering warriors, we can identify with other wives whose husbands (or vice versa) have served in harm's way.

Recently we were asked for a reference for a veteran police officer who has been on the force for over twenty years and suffers from PTSD. We were not in a position to help him personally, but we referred him to a counselor who could. Once people know who you are and what your situation is, they are more apt to come to you for help. Why? Because they want to talk to someone who has been there, done that.

Most of us of the Vietnam War era would not, and probably should not, take on the onerous responsibility of foster parenting. However, having been parents, we know families have lots of needs—even such things as diapers. Those who work with foster children and fostering parents are stretched to the max in this slow economy. Your helping hand restores their faith in the goodness of humanity.

A local church volunteers to provide transportation to doctor's appointments and grocery stores and the like. Several churches supply meals for the homeless. The point is not what you do, but that you do something. The person you serve doesn't have to be a stranger; he or she may be a family member. Knowing we care strengthens and encourages those who serve and those who are being served.

Four-year-old Daniel, the grandson of a friend, has cancer. Sometimes his blood counts are so poor that he cannot mix with other children, even the children in the same hospital ward. Cards, prayers, and consoling words carry this family through one crisis to another. This family has three other children. These parents are stretched to the max. Any show of help encourages them to persevere.

When we help someone else, we lay stepping stones making it viable for them to find healing.

Choice 4—Become Informed

I'm not talking about formal education—college degrees and all that. If college is possible, please take advantage of it, but don't eliminate informal avenues—that of simply becoming knowledgeable about the effects of trauma, especially trauma brought on by war. Most of us are dealing with someone suffering with PTSD. It is a broad topic encompassing things like anger and depression. The more we know about these topics, the more adept we can be at caring for those who suffer, most especially our spouses. The more we understand what triggers flashbacks for our warriors, the wiser we will be in avoiding them.

I like books. I like the feel of a book in my hand, but that is only one element of this broad field of education. Another source for education can be DVDs. Herein lies an ocean of opportunity. Charlie and I are working our way through a five-unit series of DVDs about PTSD. The American Association of Christian Counselors has a number of DVD series of related topics. Many of these courses come with a certificate upon completion of the course and the tests, but this follow-through is not mandatory.

This may seem a bit bizarre for someone my age, but I recently enrolled and completed a chaplaincy course. I also fully intend to take specialized training in critical incident response and crisis intervention for individuals and groups. Do I want to be a first-responder (someone who works with the police, medics, or fireman)? Do I plan to fly off to disaster scenes? Not particularly. What I do want to be is trained to effectively respond to someone in trauma. My hope is that I will contribute more effectively to the needs of warriors and their spouses. Writing this book has opened vistas to me I didn't know existed. Being informed became of paramount importance. I hope many of you will become better informed and enjoy the journey.

"Life is change. Growth is optional. Choose wisely."[126]
Karen Kaiser Clark

But when we have been made perfect and complete,
then the need for these inadequate special gifts will come to an end,
and they will disappear.
1 Corinthians 13:10

Chapter 15
Hypervigilance

Terry Balfe fears losing control of situations. "He's a control freak!" said Barbara. "With that I think comes the hypervigilance. He has to know where everyone is at every moment."

Like most and maybe all combat veterans, Erol Tuzcu struggles with hypervigilance. His wife, Susan, said. "Erol has to sit where he faces the door or with his back to a wall. I was used to that though because my dad had the same 'quirk'. I always stand and wait until he chooses his seat then I will sit down."

Hypervigilance? Always! JoAnn Moore said, "Guy hates the sound of helicopters. He still reacts to the sound of the blades."

Charlie Taylor takes that one step further. When he doesn't react to the sound of a helicopter, I'm curious as to why not. He said, "Hueys make a unique sound. I know the difference immediately." I react; he doesn't. Go figure.

Roy Moseman reacts in a similar manner. Lynne said, "Roy doesn't duck under a table when a Huey flies over the house, but he is certainly aware of the sound. He gets nervous in crowds and sometimes will need to leave and go outside. He won't sit with his back to a door and scopes out the exits of any building we are in."

When we go out to dinner, Charlie insists he have a seat facing the exits. He scans his surroundings nonstop throughout the meal. This is very typical of combat veterans.

"Dave Schoenian approaches every day always expecting an

ambush. He is always on guard and constantly looking for an escape route. Dave avoids most places and situations where confrontations might occur. He does reconnaissance in everything he does, especially where he parks his car. He is always on guard, day and night."[127]

What Is Hypervigilance?

Simply said, hypervigilance is a state of being on very high alert to possible risks or threats. It is always feeling like you must be watchful of what and who surrounds you. For Ron Miriello that means being suspicious of whoever is nearby.[128] Barbara Cannode said, "I worry that if I touch Daniel, he might overreact without realizing it." Donna Gander said, "Terry is very aware of his surroundings. He pays great attention to people, places, and things. He doesn't like for anyone to walk up behind him or stand too close behind him." And Barbara Bedell says about her husband, "For Metz hypervigilance means being super organized. He must be busy all the time. He doesn't like to fly, but when he does, he goes first class, first row.

In *Combat Trauma*, Dr. Jim Johnson calls hypervigilance "mental defibrillation—a loss of concentration where many thoughts are trying to flow through one's mind simultaneously, with none effectively progressing."[129]

The *Miller-Keane Encyclopedia and Dictionary of Medicine, Nursing, and Allied Health* says hypervigilance is "abnormally increased arousal, responsiveness to stimuli, and screening of the environment for threats[130]

Physical symptoms of hypervigilance include dilated pupils, an increased heart rate, and elevated blood pressure. It is thought that biologically this originates from cave men who developed reduced blood flow in the extremities when faced with the saber-toothed tiger. This enabled the cave man not to bleed to death should the tiger attack.

Most of the spouses interviewed for this book agree hypervigilance from their husbands include an increased startled reflex, and in a few cases include avoidance of perceived threats, even to the point of taking an alternative route to evade suspicious landscapes or buildings. Having a difficult time falling or staying asleep and feeling irritable or having bursts of anger are notable in most cases.

Most of us have experienced something frightful. When our physical alarm bells go off, we will typically do one of three things—fight, flee, or freeze. This reflex is centered in the limbic system of the brain, and is responsible for various functions within the body, including the heart rate and blood pressure. The limbic neuron trigger adrenaline into our system. In *Once a Warrior Always a Warrior*, Col. Charles W. Hoge says, "The limbic alarm system of the brain 'hijacks' the conscious rational areas in order to ensure the person's entire attention and focus in directed toward survival."[131]

Hypervigilance is taught and honed during military training and in combat situations. It is not just some overreaction by a warrior to some trigger. It's the response engrained in the psyche and sinews of every trained military man and woman. It saves their hide in the field. After the horrific events of war, it's permanently in the warrior's makeup—like a DVD played in the brain over and over and over again and again.

Common sense tells us that everyone should be vigilant; it could save your life in your home or on the streets of this nation. One day I reached into the hen's nesting area to gather eggs and felt something cold and slimy—a snake. Trust me, I leaped from the henhouse, heart racing. I'm glad it was only a bull snake and not a rattler, but I assure you I don't reach blindly into the nests anymore.

However "normal" vigilance is, it is very different from the combat learned vigilance of our warriors.

Barbe Balfe said, "I can't pretend to know all of Terry's fears but I do know some. He fears the element of surprise; therefore, he's adamant about sitting with his back to the wall facing the exit in a restaurant or sitting in the last seat of an aisle at a theatre or concert. We're able to laugh at these 'quirks' now even though they're still carried out. When I read Dr. Jim Johnson's book (*Combat Trauma: A Personal Look at Long-Term Consequences*), I found that this is a common thing among the veterans. I teased Terry and told him it's going to be a funny sight walking into the reunion and all the guys will be seated all around the room against the walls—it's gonna be kinda hard to carry on a conversation that way.

"Terry's got to know where everyone is at every moment. Some of the wives and I were laughing about this common 'quirk' last fall. Another thing I learned after reading Dr. Johnson's books—that it comes from the need to keep everyone safe—but for crying out loud! –to have to answer 'Where did you go?' for the nth time….I'm not talking about going somewhere in the car by myself! That would never happen. This happens when I've only gone to the backyard or basement or even to the bathroom. After a while it starts to weigh on you."

None of the spouses will change or want to change the warrior's attitude toward hypervigilance. Here are three reasons we believe hypervigilance plays a significant role in their lives: 1) It has been drilled into them during their training. It is indelibly written in their memory banks,2) It kept them alive in combat, and 3) It keeps us alive and well on the home front. For those reasons, we will go with the flow. We may at times feel a bit frustrated with the comment, "Mistakes will get you killed," but they are right and we know it. We are grateful for their diligence on our behalf.

Trekking On—One Day at a Time

In January of 2004, Charlie Taylor had open-heart surgery. Much of the damage to his heart muscle was the residual effect of Agent Orange, a chemical used to defoliate the jungles of Vietnam. Over the next nine months four additional surgeries followed, all different, and nothing compared to the initial surgery. The fifth and final operation required the reopening of the chest wall. Not only had a staph infection set in, but it appeared the sternum had been compromised and amputation (or a partial amputation) would be necessary in order to eradicate the spread of infection.

Like so many things in this life when all was over, we had good news and bad news. The good news was that the infection had not compromised his sternum and amputation was unnecessary. The bad news—the chest walls contained four, not just one, pockets of staphylococcus. Had we not gone through the surgery, he would have died from the infection. His condition had been a time bomb.

I learned something from that year-long ordeal. First, God can be TRUSTED regardless of our circumstances. Second, we must be ever vigilant when it come to matters of our well-being. Real danger to our health and happiness may be more unseen than seen. Mistakes and inattention may kill you. Third, I learned that healing comes in time, but the scars never disappear. The twelve-inch scar on Charlie's chest will forever be a reminder of his physical and emotional trauma.

Mistakes Will Get You Killed

If I (Diana) have heard that comment once, I've heard it a million times. Barbe Balfe says, "Not only does he say mistakes will get you killed, but he will follow that comment with 'If you were in the field right now, you'd be dead.'"

No question about it—"Mistakes will get you killed." For Sam, our younger son, that became an issue when he did a poor job of cutting the grass. I assured Charlie that mowing the grass wasn't in the same category as fighting the war in Vietnam. From Charlie's perspective, remembering such things as the battle at "Snoopy's Nose" and many other battles, this truism has been indelibly imprinted on his memory. On September 15, 1967, his unit boarded small Navy landing crafts and proceeded to ferry to a predetermined spot where they hoped to engage the enemy. But the enemy was lying in wait for the column of sixteen boats laden with troops. A ferocious battle went from morning into the night with many killed and wounded.

When Charlie and his men were finally able to disembark onto the riverbanks, the enemy was all around them. He called in artillery to within twenty-five meters of their position, killing many of the enemy. Had a "mistake" been made, it would have been Charlie's soldiers who would have been killed.

In 2004, now many years since the war, this message was driven home to me as we journeyed through the quagmire of Charlie's health and well-being. If we had not been hypervigilant, he'd be dead. As I related previously our experience to that of the warriors, two factors stand out. First is the significance of their training. Mistakes and inattention to detail may get you killed. Being vigilant is drilled into the mind and muscle of every recruit. Hypervigilance is an absolute on the battlefield. It, like one's weapon, must be part and parcel to the warrior's gear and readiness. Similar to Charlie's open-heart surgery, real danger may be more unseen than seen. And second, like surgery, the effects of war leave deep, ugly scars—scars that never disappear and may be carefully hidden, only to be revealed to those whom the warrior feels he can truly trust.

Mistakes can get you killed. Hypervigilance may keep you alive. Scanning our surroundings and being sensitive to danger just may save your life and the lives of those you love. So, while some of us roll our eyes when we hear our well-meaning warriors repeatedly use the statement—mistakes will get you killed—I suggest we take the message to heart. If we want to be safe and whole and have the opportunity to grow old, which is a prize worth pursuing, we must be vigilant.

Kind words are a creative force,
A power that concurs in the building up of all that is good,
And energy that showers blessings upon the world.
Lawrence G. Lovasik

CHAPTER 16
The Silent Wounds Of Combat
Memories, Concentration, Numbness, Withdrawal

"Roy Moseman learned very early after his return from Vietnam to turn off emotions in a second. 'My family thinks that I don't care, but it's my way of handling it. I will completely shut out the problem until I am alone and can rationally think about how to handle it. After Vietnam, I went for years without emotions. Nothing made me happy and nothing made me sad. I just turned off my emotions. If not, I would not have been able to survive.'"[132]

It took many years for Lynne Moseman to understand his trauma. Roy said, "Lynne has put up with more from me than I would have ever put up with. She has taken the mood swings, the verbal abuse, the anger, the depression, and everything else. It has been very hard on her and I love her so much for trying to understand what I have and am going through."[133]

Recently, Lynne shared this: "I guess the best coping skill I've learned is to share and talk about my feelings. I've been blessed with some very loving girlfriends who act as my mental health counselors. For years we didn't have a name for whatever was troubling Roy. I didn't know how to handle his behavior and was embarrassed to admit Roy and I were having issues in our marriage. We finally put the pieces together and learned that the symptoms of PTSD were describing Roy to the 'T'. It was comforting to know that there is a name for what has been torturing my husband for all these years and we were not alone. Roy's PTSD group at our local VA, medication, and—on my part—a lot of prayers have made a huge difference in our lives. I'm also thankful that our son, Michael, has a better understanding of his father's behavior. I'm not saying it is always easy, but we have both learned not to take Roy's harsh words personally. There is much more information out there to help people with PTSD and their families to live with it. I just wish we had access to it years ago."

In time each surviving warrior's tour of duty ended. They rotated home. They hoped to pick up their lives where they had left off, but that rarely happened. Many came home broken by the horrors of war to a country, to former friends, and sometimes to family members who treated them like they were the enemy. So they stuffed their painful memories inside their heads, hearts, and guts, and did their best to move on with life.

Nice idea, but it didn't work for most of them. After countless encounters with the virulent society and nonresponsive Veterans Administration, they ceased resisting. Their flares of anger and frustration numbed, and they withdrew from society. They worked, they came home, and they repeated that routine until the day they could legitimately leave the workforce.

Some warriors simply crawled into a protective shell and hid their feelings in hard work. Charlie Taylor shut out his experiences like someone might shut a book. It was nothing for him to work fifty and sixty hours a week and spend the weekend hunting and fishing. Others, like Ron Miriello, became defensive and stood up to the lies and backlash of society.

Debbie Miriello says this about Ron: "Like too many others, Ron just wants to feel like he can handle it all by himself. And in his case, his work actually helped him, as he worked as a veteran's counselor and then as a college administrator. He continued counseling veterans throughout his career and says that counseling them and crying with them is what helped him the most. He had a successful career. He retired a few years ago and now presents a PowerPoint presentation on the Vietnam War to many groups, especially service groups.

What are these silent wounds of war? They are horrific <u>memories,</u>

the inability to <u>concentrate,</u> <u>numbness,</u> and <u>withdrawal</u>—internal emotional lacerations from the nefarious evils of combat borne by our brave warriors.

Memories

Memories are often in Technicolor and the DVD seldom stops running. In *Once a Warrior, Always a Warrior*, Dr. Charles W. Hoge says, "Memories of life-threatening events are not stored in the same parts of the brain as other memories or thoughts. They are stored in deeper areas within the brain called the 'limbic system,' which controls survival reflexes and connects directly to areas involving all of the basic functions of the body necessary for survival, including adrenaline, breathing, heart rate, and muscle tone."[134]

Memories? Yes, indelibly written on the brain—the smells, the sounds, the sights—nothing appears to have changed from that day until today. Yet it seems more accurate to note that the limbic area compresses and stores events. While it may be impossible to erase these memories, it is possible to suppress the intensity and frequency of them. Thus the warrior may build a tolerance level when memories explode in their conscious minds. Hopefully their reaction to the trauma may become less acute over time and with psychological treatment.

Mary Galde said, "For years Dan's memories were too painful to talk about. He didn't want to remember any of it or go over any of it in his mind. He has spent a lifetime trying to forget. Sadly, I think there is either the feeling that if he opens up to seriously talk about it, the horror will come back. Or, if he talks about it, he fears he will break down and, God forbid, exhibit weakness. Better to just stuff and store."

When Dan Canode came home, he had many jobs, none of which he kept very long. He probably will not admit it, but most he quit after a disagreement. Then he worked for a bank in Toledo for about fifteen years. Unfortunately, they moved out of town in 1997. Eventually he was forced to quit work because he could not control his PTSD.

"Erol Tuzcu continues to have raging periods of sadness when he recalls an event of February 20, 1969, in Kien Hoa Province. As the helicopters dropped the troops, the landing zone proved to be very hot as the enemy opened up from several sides."

Erol said, "The feel, sights, and smells and the horror that occurred after we landed was to be with me the rest of my life. Several 105mm rounds had been rigged as booby traps and each time one would explode, several brothers would be hit. My buddy Mirick tripped one of the rounds blowing off both of his legs. I applied tourniquets and continued to dodge bullets but Mirick bled to death with me lying next to him."[135]

Yes, memories…

Concentration

In *Combat Trauma*, Dr. James Johnson compares the similarities between a diseased heart, resulting in defibrillation causing improper blood flow to the body, and "mental defibrillation—a loss of concentration where many thoughts are trying to flow through one's mind simultaneously, with none effectively progressing."[136]

Concentrating and maintaining focus may become a common malady among many warriors after their wartime experience. When on the battlefield, their attention was highly focused. Knowing every detail of the terrain, every sound, every movement was essential for survival. At those times, high levels of adrenaline and stress hormones poured into their bodies. The body was on full alert. Shutting it down for less demanding circumstances may become very difficult. To focus on something other than survival after returning home was most likely a difficult challenge.

"Roy Moseman has a very difficult time reading because after a page or two, his mind is off somewhere else. Often after reading three or four pages, he has no idea what he has read. 'I have to really concentrate or be very interested in whatever I read. Also, I will be in a conversation with someone and the next thing I know I am thinking of something entirely different. That can be very embarrassing, but I can't seem to help it.'"[137]

"Prolonged thoughts of our combat trauma can also lead to loss of short-term memory. Dave Schoenian cannot retain a name, even after it has just been told to him. 'Driving has become a hazard, my mind wanders, I forget where I am going, and I don't see what is going on in front of me. This frightens my wife to death.'"[138]

Stop, look, and listen. That's what we tell our children and grandchildren when we need to cross the street. It's equally good advice when we navigate our routine throughout the day. Know where you are. Decide what to do next. Then make your move.

If and when our minds wander aimlessly, we give ourselves permission to come back into the present. Experts call it "mindfulness." To be mindful, we simply practice being aware of the present moment without judgment or expectation. In other words, we stop and take notice of this very moment. Be cognizant of your breathing. Think about something that brings you joy and a sense of peace. Take as long as it takes to become calm and feel in control. Let us ask ourselves if we can learn from this event. Tomorrow we will try again. Equally important—let us be kind to ourselves.

Numbness

The battle of February 26-27, 1968, where most of Co B, 3/60th Infantry battalion were either killed or wounded has been documented previously. Guy P. Moore says of that battle, he lost so many friends that he feels he was never 'right in the head' again. He became a loner and had no desire to make new friends or ever get close to anyone again."[139]

An unspoken element of training in the military is not to show emotions. During combat, the warrior turns off his emotions and operates on trained instinct. That is not macho; it is survival, but when the warrior returns to society, he finds it difficult to turn off his training and his memories and connect to others, even four decades later.

"Very soon after returning from Vietnam, I (Jim Johnson) realized that emotionally, I must stuff my feelings. There was no one with whom to discuss what had happened to me, as most of the other people at my new assignment had no idea what it was like to live the life of a grunt daily."[140]

"Dave Schoenian came home to learn that 'Vietnam' was a dirty word. Finally he just quit talking about it to those who were not veterans."[141]

Most of us have had an electrocardiogram (ECG or EKG)— that

records the electrical impulses of the heart and to the professional's eye will show either a normal heart rhythm or a disorder. If there is no rhythm (has flatlined), the person is dead. When an individual suffers from emotional numbness, he or she has no emotional impulses. He or she has emotionally flatlined. Feelings of happiness or unhappiness may not even exist.

It may well be that numbness is the results of unrequited grief or fear. Acts of killing or be killed under war conditions are expected, but after the war, the trauma becomes overwhelming. It is too much to bear. So, the warrior shuts his feelings away. Withdrawal from interacting with other people is just a step away from numbness.

Withdrawal

"Since I (Dave Schoenian) started going to MRFA reunions in '93, and later 47th Regiment reunions, I realized that I was more comfortable, and felt safer, in the company of combat veterans. I left work in 2002, and had been going to the local Vet Center for two years. I joined our Purple Heart Chapter in 1999, and this along with the Vet Center became my two main choices of public interaction. This is not to say I didn't go places and do things. I just didn't join, attend, or take part in activities that didn't have a military base. To this day it is the same. I have built a perimeter around my house (mentally) and made it my base camp. I am lucky as there are six Nam vets in my block. I spend more time with my dog than anyone else. I have made a family out of my brothers at the Vet Center, and like them we chose each other to TRUST and be close to. I am still the platoon sergeant. I do commit to my responsibilities of being a father and grandfather. I have never ever not accepted and cherished those responsibilities. I go and speak at various functions proudly representing veterans. Once a week, I go to a local bar, which is owned by a Marine in my group. Along with others from the group we have our own therapy. I drink Sprite. Ella and I go to Disney World two or three times a year; we bought into their vacation club which gives us a better, less congested accommodation. I have learned how to recon areas for safety and ways to get in and out. I have joined a group called Project Healing Waters for disabled service-connected veterans, teaching fly fishing as therapy.

My group at the Vet Center is now my platoon.

"Just like in Nam, the guys are dying. Then you remember why you were afraid to get too close personally with people, but for me I had to know all the names, take care of the men. And I still do it, as these men today rely on me. They know I am there for them 24/7. I love them.

"I like being a loner, and just want to be left the @&*! alone, to ride out the time I have left. My way! My house is big enough that Ella and I have space to have our own times. My dog is my very best pal. We very seldom have friends over, mainly just grandkids. Ella has one very good friend, Nancy, she used to work with, but rarely sees. I try to get her out of the house when I can, but with her deteriorated health condition, she is 100 percent dependent on me.

"We went to Disney World recently. The Mosemans came with us. This is a big step for us, sharing our special time. But there again he is my Brother from Nam, and such a special friend, we wanted to share that time with the both of them to help make their holidays."

Many warriors withdrew from society. Conditions at home, in the neighborhood, and at work were more tolerable if they left their past locked in a closet. Life was a bit less complicated that way. They felt safer. In reality, that wasn't the case. They couldn't hide. One never knew when a flashback might be triggered and their bodies and minds would go into autopilot and they would respond much like they would have in Vietnam when under attack. Still, withdrawal was a way of self-medicating, and most warriors used it successfully for quite some time."

JoAnne Moore said, "I found an occupation that allows me to make friends because Guy doesn't want to mingle with people. But, recently he has opened up a bit. He feels most comfortable with other Vietnam veterans, most especially Joe, my brother-in-law, who is also a Vietnam veteran. Joe talked Guy into attending a meeting with other Vietnam vets. That brought about a more open exchange between Guy and me."

Silent Wounds—Past Wounds Tweak the Present

Amy's husband, Bob, an Army officer, has been deployed to Iraq twice. Amy knows what it is to maintain a happy home as a solo parent to her three children when Bob has been deployed and as a "buffer" parent when Bob is home. One of those buffer times occurred when her five-year-old son, Ty, cried over his broken bike.

"Is someone shooting at you?" asked Bob.

"No." Ty shakes his head.

"Then I think you're having a good day," says good ol' dad.

Amy is livid. "You need to cut this out right now!"

"What?" Bob asked.

"Stop treating everyone that way."

"What way?"

"Like everything we say is stupid and irrelevant."

"I didn't say that," says Bob.

"No," says Amy. "But you completely invalidate anything Ty says. And you keep doing it."

"Well, I just don't see why he cares about something as stupid as a bike when people are dying."

"He cares because he is five, and thank God, he doesn't know people are dying. I'd like to keep it that way as long as possible if you don't mind. You serve in the military to protect us, right? To protect our children's innocence?"

Bob nods.

"Then value their innocence!"

"I didn't think of it like that."

"Well, you're gonna start thinking of it like that or I'm going to be doing a lot more yelling."

"Gotcha."

~~*

Memories, concentration, numbness, and withdrawal—I think of it as the silent residuals of war. From the point of view of the beholder, the warrior looks like he has life put together, but from inside the head of the combat veteran, nothing could be farther from the truth. Horrific memories of war, injuries, and death negatively affect their ability to concentrate. Feelings of guilt and grief which may manifest itself in anger, nightmares, and hyperalertness may be so tightly packaged that the warrior becomes numb to his deeply buried emotions. When such is the case, the warrior withdraws, and when the warrior withdraws, the spouse and family feel ignored, frozen out, or simply pushed aside as if they are looking at a family photo and are not a part of the picture. They feel isolated from the warrior they love.

Many spouses and families have been confronted with the "silent" trauma of war—memory and concentration issues coupled with numbness and withdrawal. The question is, what do we do about it? And how can we protect ourselves from becoming secondary victims? Here are a few ideas...

Archway 1—Patient Patients

Many of our warriors receive treatment from professional counselors. Some are active in group therapy. From a "keystone" perspective, we know that we must be patient with the patient and with ourselves. It may well be worth our effort.

In this "archway" I want to draw your attention to two types of therapy—EMDR and MBCT. I have personally gone through EMDR. After several sessions, I felt a switch had just been turned inside my head. Both therapies have been successfully used in the treatment of PTSD.

EMDR – Eye Movement Desensitization and Reprocessing Therapy. EMDR has been used with individuals who have suffered from unresolved trauma. It is also used to treat children.

MBCT—Mindfulness-Based Cognitive Behavior Therapy. It is a positive approach to eliminating negative thinking and behavior patterns that is often associated with PTSD.

Earlier in this chapter we defined "mindfulness" as being aware of the present moment without judgment or expectation. It is the practice of bringing your awareness deliberately into the present moment. The dictionary defines "cognitive" as relating to or as being conscious of our intellectual activities—such as thinking, reasoning, imagining, or remembering. In essence, then, MBCT helps those who are suffering from trauma to be aware of the present and not focused on the past or the future. In so doing, the sufferer will be more apt to manage the current stress and stressors with a more flexible and accepting mindset.

Archway 2 – Healing Journeys

There are several other practical ways to handle PTSD. I've listed two, but there are others which deserve recognition. *Project Healing Waters* was brought to my attention by Dave Schoenian. He has greatly benefited from it.

This is therapy for me (Dave Schoenian). We started in the fall of 2013. We now have attendees from Ohio, WV, and PA. The fellow that leads the group is a divorced veteran. He needed something to do, talked to the local Vet Center, and is able to use their facility for meetings. Many volunteers come and instruct us including classes at the local Cabelas. I have been away from fishing for many years. Never did fly fish. Now I am a guy who is not going to put 1000s of dollars in this, but I did buy all the basic items. Tying flies is great, but I have decided to buy mine. We have many classes on fly tying, knots, what to use for each season, etc. We went to a gym at a local school (in winter) to practice casting. *Healing Waters* puts on a major event at special locations and we get to participate, one guy at a session. I haven't gone yet. I choose to let those who really need it more than me go first. I have gone with my son-in-law to lower WV into the mountains to fish, and am going again next week. This is a great experience, but requires patience, which I am working on. He is also a vet and a state trooper, so it works for him too.

Last year my very good friend from my Vet Center group, and also in this class, had a heart attack midway through our year. He was supposed to go on one of the special outings. The day he got out of the hospital we were having a practice fishing session at a local state park pond. He made his wife bring him that evening because this means so much to him. I told our leader, there is your success. Base this group on him, how much it means to him, and discount those who quit coming. This is the same for our Vet Center group, we are one big family of sixteen to eighteen combat vets who love and depend on each other.

We have class Wednesday night, my daughter is coming. We are going to have a fund raiser in May. So you see it is not how I feel, but how the rest of them feel. This is my goal, being platoon sergeant again. I will say this, I wish I would have done this earlier when my eyes were better. It is so peaceful. I just want to carry a weapon, and you can't. Anything that gives these vets peace of mind, I'm for.

Project Healing Waters began in 2005 serving wounded military service members at Walter Reed Army Medical Center. For a program to exist it must be staffed by volunteers from the fly fishing club, have available a DOD or VA medical facility willing to host the program, and, of course, injured military members or disabled veterans willing to participate. See their website for more information: https://www.projecthealingwaters.org/

Operation Wolfhound is an organization that trains wolfhounds as service dogs for veterans who suffer from PTSD. It is an international program based in Tucson, Arizona. This nonprofit connects vets with PTSD and psychiatric service dogs for free. The program focuses on Russian wolfhounds, also known as borzois, large dogs with a long life span, and an independent personality.

Bandit, a borzois, belongs to Captain Ken Costich, a Vietnam warrior and acquaintance. A small portion of his story has been included in this book. Bandit is a handsome dog to be sure, but more importantly, he is Costich's lifeline. He knows when Costich is having a nightmare. He senses when Costich is overly stressed and in his quiet way brings peace into Costich's world. Costich said, "I feel safe with him." For more information, check out Operation Wolfhound at https://www.facebook.com/OperationWolfhound4vets

Numerous other programs of this nature are available. Not enough good can be said for alternative therapy such as art therapy and equine therapy. Several universities have explored farming and gardening. Perhaps you feel called to support one of these nonprofit organizations. I pray so.

Archway 3—Optimism

Optimism is "a mental attitude or world view that interprets situations and events as being best (optimized)." It is the tendency to see the positive side, to see life and the future in a favorable light. This does not imply that we see life through rose-colored glasses, but that we see and determine to make and take good our present circumstances.

Research garnered from Mayo Clinic says positive thinking is linked to a wide range of health benefits including:

- Longer life span
- Less stress
- Lower rates of depression
- Increased resistance to the common cold
- Better stress management and coping skills
- Lower risk of cardiovascular disease-related death
- Increased physical well-being
- Better psychological health[142]

Optimistic people usually have better health and live longer. Surely they are more pleasant to be around. One study suggests that optimistic people find pleasure in what they do. Regardless of the job, they find aspects that are pleasant.

If you want to build your optimistic outlook, try this: 1) make friends with optimistic outlooks; 2) each day write down three good things that have happened to you; 3) repeat affirming comments to yourself daily; 4) catch pessimistic thoughts quickly and turn them around. Optimistic thinkers tend to be happier than their pessimistic counterparts.

Let us choose optimism at the core of our being, starting with gratitude to those who have done their best to bring a ray of happiness into our lives. Our warriors have not forgotten the war. The images, the smells, the noise wrestling inside their heads are their memories of real life experiences. Love and compassion bridges the canyon between pain and possibility. Indeed, let us love and show kindness. We can do this. Let us nurture optimism!

Archway 4—Teach and Be Teachable

To teach and be teachable implies verbal communication and most certainly that is how most of us understand these concepts. I believe we teach and learn through several methods, primarily through spoken exchanges, but also through listening, reading, and by visible actions. Let's look more closely at verbal and nonverbal communication.

Dr. Albert Mehrabian, author of *Silent Messages,* is quoted to have said that only 7 percent of any message is communicated through words. On the other hand, 93 percent of what we express is done nonverbally. To further delineate, he said that 38 percent of nonverbal is done through vocal elements and 55 percent through facial expressions, posture, and gestures. Others have said that 60 to 90 percent is nonverbal which means that the spoken word is a small percentage of our vocal exchanges.

Regardless of the percentages, we see that it is not so much what we say, but how we say it. In addition to that, the old adage "Actions speak louder than words" plays a significant role in how our messages are received. However, we should never underestimate the power of our words which may influence the listener for good or for ill. Consider this, whether we are sending a message either by verbal or by nonverbal means, there is one overriding consideration—attitude. Our attitude conveyed by words, spoken and unspoken, and our deeds will make or break a relationship. Knowing that may make us more conscious of our communication skills and stimulate us to become better communicators.

Last year, we purchased a butterfly kit which included fuzzy caterpillars in a small glass jar. The day came when these wiggly worms hatched into butterflies and we released them. While we waited for them to mature into monarch butterflies, we watched an educational film and learned much about the life and migration of monarchs. I was as much the student as the teacher.

As "keystones" our mental and physical well-being is often challenged to the point of exhaustion. Could it be that we are able to fill our love-cups by becoming the teacher and the student regardless of the complexity or simplicity of the lesson? Not only did I learn something about butterflies and enjoy the process, but the day-by-day observation distracted me from the woes of life.

Teaching often comes to us through lectures, but not always. Sometimes it's teaching by example. To do so means we need to not just listen, but to truly hear what the other person is saying. Our ability to hear validates the person we are communicating with. When we validate someone, we are being teachable.

Listening validates the person, the message, and the emotion of the one speaking. When we are teaching, we must not forget to listen to the student. If the student doesn't understand our message, we are not connecting. If we are not hearing the verbal, nonverbal, and the emotion of the student, we are not communicating. We might just as well shut ourselves in a locked closet. We teach by listening to our students. And when we are the students, we listen. Listen! Listen! Listen! Good teachers listen.

We all know the old story—God gave us one mouth and two ears. Therefore, we should listen twice as much and speak half as often. Keep in mind that what we do for others comes home to us. We want to be heard, so let us practice the art of listening.

Don't forget to smile! I am convinced that a cheerful countenance benefits both the listener and the speaker.

In *Smile for No Good Reason*, Dr. Lee Jampolsky says, "Practice active listening and other people will feel loved and accepted by you. And you will feel like you were just given wings."[143]

In Conclusion

A dear friend who had suffered all her adult life with the painful aftereffects of polio once said, "Pain is inevitable; misery is optional." Not a day went by without pain, yet she filled her life with laughter, music, teaching, and mentoring people like me. I will ever be grateful for the impact she has had on my life. And what a joy it is to work on this writing project with her son, Dan Galde, who—after a long career as a Pararescueman in the Air Force and some very strategic and scary assignments in Vietnam—suffers from PTSD. Also, allow me to pay tribute to the men and women who have contributed to this book. They know pain, and they strive, and most of the time succeed, to live above the misery. It is our wish—our prayer—that you who suffer from the wounds of war will find a pathway through your pain and overcome your misery.

It's like this: when I was a child
I spoke and thought and reasoned as a child does.
But when I became a man my thoughts grew
Far beyond those of my childhood,
And now I have put away the childish things.
1 Corinthians 13:11

CHAPTER 17

Aging
"Aging is not lost youth but a new stage of opportunity and strength."

Betty Friedan

Let's face it. We of the Vietnam era are getting older. We walk a little slower, our hair is either falling out or turning gray, and we hit the rack a little earlier than we used to—well, some of us do. In spite of all that, we espouse some positives. One of the most pleasing things I see is we are walking a little taller. Our shoulders are straight and we are proud of who we are, where we've been, and what we've done. Others may not like our opinions, but by golly, they are based on experience, both good and bad.

Aging—somewhere within the chronological movement between birth and old age—is a process called maturation. I like to think of it as a journey during which we mellow and master what is truly meaningful. Having done so, we can appreciate fully our senior years. Aging is not something to fear, but embrace. While some may think of it as a pageant of beauty like a rose opening its petals to the sun and the rain with equal acceptance, others will not. In fact, for the combat veteran, life may at times be more like the soggy, sucking mud through which they traversed in Vietnam. And yet, as we age, many have nurtured perspicaciously their outlook on life, and many can understand and discern that which is truly noteworthy about their passage of years.

Perhaps the most meaningful benefit we receive as we age is perspective. Experience gained personally or from listening and learning from others often gives us a more balanced view of the past, the present, and the future.

On July 22, 2013, my beloved warrior (Charlie Taylor) turned 71 years old. The Vietnam War was forty-six years ago. Those passing years have been kind to Charlie. He can still do most anything he puts his mind to. He enjoys life and plans to work indefinitely. However, a year ago he was forced by law to initiate his Social Security retirement payments, and it jolted him from his moorings. He took a long look at his physical and psychological well-being and set some goals to regain muscle tone and determine to retain mental cognition. It strengthened his ambition to be all that he can be, including taking good care of his wife. He also got hooked on Facebook.

Another benefit of aging is perseverance. Whether the years have passed unkindly or gracefully, we and our warriors have persevered. Yes, aging brings multidimensional change to one's physical, psychological, and social well-being. As the clock ticks, the body tocks. Change is inevitable. How we deal with aging is, in most cases, a matter of preferences and choices. Congratulate yourself—we've made it thus far; let us pursue the future with determination

Barbara Cannode (Daniel Cannode) puts it this way: "'It' has impacted our relationship. We have had a very hard walk through life, as have many of the families and spouses of PTSD veterans. I am at a point in my life where I am glad that what I feel is that the really hard years have finally passed. We are now going to hopefully just continue to heal and forgive each other. You see, as much as I know that the war was—and is—our great burden to carry, we both have lashed out in anger as we all know it takes two to fight. Dan just has more demons to let go of."

Barbara and Daniel, like many, have persevered. They have set their relationship as a priority, and they have persisted through the good times and the stressful times.

Like most Vietnam veterans, Charlie is proud of his service. It played a significant part in creating the person he has become. Those military skills and leadership abilities that came to the forefront under the stress of battle strengthened his character and have come to his assistance in making decisions and building a successful business. But let's face it: he isn't the svelte warrior at seventy-one years of age that he was when he was twenty-five. Things change. The reflexive muscles of the body, the agility of the mind, and the resilience of the spirit—they all modify over time.

The Vietnam War was forty-plus years ago, yet it lives on in the hearts and minds of the veteran today. How we make peace with our limitations, and how we savor the preciousness of life and living together, is most often a matter of choice. I believe life is for making memories; let's make them good ones. The daily routines of life may be one of escalating drama and disease. Many of the veterans tell us that coping with the past became a range of unscaled, uncharted mountains in the present.

"Terry," Barbe Balfe said, "hasn't changed his attitude about his time in Vietnam, but getting back with his fellow soldiers has made it easier for him to reflect on a few things."

Not one of the families I've spoken with has lived in utopia. They have had struggles and joys. The one overriding characteristic in each case is resiliency. Life has not been a cakewalk, but a marathon. Endurance has been a challenge. Life does not always appear to be as readable and consistent as we would like. It may not register like an EKG where lines go up and down consistently in a rhythmic, measurable motion as we would expect from a normal healthy heart. Sometimes it appears erratic, jumping up and down all over the page—as if we are having a heart attack.

We started this chapter with a pithy statement from Betty Friedan. Allow me to repeat it: "Aging is not lost youth, but a new stage of opportunity and strength." Let us pursue that thought as we explore what it means to have a healthy future.

Healthy Aging
Physiological Well-being

What do I mean by healthy aging? Most certainly, we will address the big three—food, rest, and exercise. But from an all-encompassing point of view, we must look at the psychological, physiological, and the spiritual—the whole person approach.

According to *Healthy Aging for Dummies*[144], there are four major health concerns in which we who are aging should take special interest: cancer, cardiovascular disease, diabetes, and osteoporosis. Cancer is one of the top causes of death worldwide. Most Vietnam combat veterans have no control over the effects of Agent Orange which contributes to a variety of diseases, most especially heart and diabetes—two very good reasons most of us want to work on becoming and staying healthy.

Good eating habits, sufficient sleep, and regular exercise are significant contributors to physical well-being. Eight hours of sleep a night is recommended. We need sufficient sleep for both psychological and physiological reasons. "The body uses this time for healing and growth, and your body produces many hormones essential for proper function during the deepest sleep stages."[145] Lack of sleep contributes to all kinds of diseases such as cardiovascular, depression, and diabetes. We will look again at sleep and the ramifications of it in chapter 18 at which time we will consider the problems of nightmares.

Exercise should be weight-bearing—not necessarily strenuous, but definitely consistent. Most of us tend to gain weight as we age. My doctor told me that not only do we gain weight, but we redistribute it and not necessarily in the right places. "Approximately 30 illnesses and diseases are linked to being overweight."[146] Some believe that being just a little overweight can contribute to health issues. "According to the *Journal of the American Medical Association*, obesity is the second-leading cause of preventable death in the U.S., right after smoking."[147]

Our exercise goal should be thirty minutes every day. Things affected by exercise or lack of it are arthritis, cardiovascular disease, diabetes (especially type 2, non-insulin-dependent), high blood pressure, sleep apnea, and strokes. Certain cancers are also indirectly affected by exercise. "National Cancer Institute experts concluded that obesity is associated with cancers of the colon, breast (postmenopausal), endometrium (the lining of the uterus), kidney, and esophagus."[148]

My last blood analysis showed a slight rise in my sugar levels. This was a surprise as I've always been on the low-level, and yet it wasn't as I love carbohydrates—especially the sweet kind. I'm far from being a saint in this arena, but I have become more conscious about the kind of wheat and sugar content of my purchases. When we eat out, I've learned to ask for sweet potatoes rather than white potatoes. I jokingly say that when I get to heaven, I'll eat what I want, when I want, and as much as I want. In the meantime, I guess I'll stick with the rules of healthy eating, and I hope you will too.

Psychological Well-being

We've talked a bit about the physiological benefits of exercise, but what about the psychological benefits? Not only do most Americans not get enough sleep and exercise, we live high-stress lifestyles. Imagine walking into our clothes closet which is crammed full of a good and bad assortment of clothes. Some of our favorite garments are there. Yet other things are totally outmoded. Some are too big, others too small, some are stained, and others in various dilapidated conditions. Definitely needs an overhaul. Stress is like that. Some is good and too much is horrible. A little stress may be good. Too much stress amputates our effectiveness.

For instance, guilt can serve a positive purpose. It may spur you to action. You may do those chores you have put off or read that book your friend loaned you and you need to return. On the other hand, guilt may lead to unforgiveness—unforgiveness of someone else or of yourself. We talked more about forgiveness in chapter 10, but as a review, let's say that forgiveness can be a tremendous stress buster. Sometimes forgiveness is like chemo treatments. Although they are hard on the body when you are going through them, they cure the cancer and in the long run bring healing.

Another stressor that has a plus-and-minus effect on the body is fear. A little fear keeps us alive, but too much doles hormones into the body that can bring long-range damage to our health. No one can deny the tremendous fear our warriors felt over the twelve months they served in Vietnam. It made little difference whether they were on their bunk or in the field. It was twelve months of stress from hell that played havoc on their immune system and on their psychological well-being. That is now history for our warriors, but we see and feel the stress that has pummeled their psyche. So, why do we choose to live high-stress lives? It seems to be innate to humans. What then can we do to reduce the stress in our lives and thus avoid future physical and psychological damage to ourselves?

We know that exercise releases endorphins "which has a healing effect on the body and mind and protects against some of the harmful effects of stress."[149] Here are a few stress-relief suggestions: swimming, walking, yoga, stationary bike ride, and just about anything that makes you move for a consistent amount of time.

Let's look at a few other stress-busters. One would be to <u>stop juggling your routine</u>. Women are great at multitasking. We can guard our children, cook a meal, watch TV, talk on the phone, and sort the mail without a pause. Yep! One of those days when we could simplify merely by expecting less from ourselves. Chores will get done and if they don't, so be it. Decide what is most important and start and finish that task before you go to the next item. Cousin to this suggestion is the art of setting boundaries. It's okay to let the answering machine catch the incoming call. Why not leave your phone in your purse and your purse in the closet?

One of the most fascinating stress-busters I found in my research was "<u>Think Globally</u>."[150] In essence, we are encouraged to change our perspective. While we complain about the dirty windows, think about the millions who have no place to live. Imagine the trauma the tsunami in Japan brought to its society. Then pause and say thanks for all you have. Change your perspective. Appreciate what you have and where you are. Could things be better for us? Are there things we would like to change? Absolutely. Just put it into perspective. Drop the small stuff in an imaginary trashcan. Put the "desired want" on tomorrow's or next month's to-do list. Ask if it will matter in a year, or a month, or a week. Barbara Johnson helps keep Jim centered by reminding him that if there is no blood involved, then it can't be all bad.

Perhaps high on our list of concerns is the search for <u>keeping our brain young.</u> No one I know wants to have Alzheimer's or some other form of dementia. Having been down this path with Charlie's mother, I can assure you this is a serious concern and deserves immediate attention. There are ways to prevent age-related memory loss.

Here's a list of ideas for good brain health given by Brent Agin, MD and Sharon Perkins, RN. Drink in moderation. Stop smoking. Manage your stress levels. For some of you, that sounds like a lot of don'ts, so on the upside, eat brain food—protein, carbohydrates, and fats. (For clarification on this topic, purchase these authors' book *Healthy Aging for Dummies*.[151])

Agin and Perkins suggest other ways to stimulate your brain and keep it young, including exercising your mind by doing such things as playing a musical instrument or doing crossword puzzles. Take up a hobby. Staying physically active is essential to our enjoyment of our senior years. One of the reasons I liked this book—and most books from the "Dummies Series"—is that it clearly lays out the information I'm most interested in. Many thanks to Brent Agin and Sharon Perkins for the depth of information which was easy to grasp and plainly written in their book on healthy aging.

Spiritual Well-being

We are multidimensional—physical, psychological, spiritual, and relational. We have looked at the physical and mental/emotional side of humanity. Now let's look at the spiritual side of mankind. Think of the spiritual as your core or your heart.

Barbe Balfe said, "It's hard to fix a broken spirit, and I would never pretend I could do so. I pray a lot and ask for spiritual guidance to show me what to do or what to say and even how to ask to make Terry's outlook on life more positive. But mostly I pray for him to be able to feel the simple joy of life itself. Just waking up on any given day can bring pure joy and he's yet to feel that. Not too long ago we were going through a very sad and trying family crisis. Terry asked me, 'How do you do it? How do you get through these times without losing it?'

"I pray a lot…sometimes all night," Barbe told Terry. "I shed many tears in the shower."

I (Diana) often couple my prayer with Scripture reading which brings me great comfort, especially that gleaned from the psalmist. It gives me a sense of walking with the Power of eternity. While we live on this earth, we will most assuredly have trials, but we are not alone. We have a great God.

Many people find prayer to be a spiritual experience with immeasurable support. It's a means of seeking consolation from God or, as they say in alcohol and drug treatment programs, a higher power. Prayer and meditation are generic to many of the religions of the world—which brings me to the concept of "mindfulness." Mindfulness is often associated with relaxation and meditation. Shamash Alidina defines it as, "the development of awareness of your inner and outer experiences, whatever they are, with a sense of kindness, curiosity and acceptance."[152] A book written by Mark Williams and Danny Penman entitled *Mindfulness: An Eight-Week Plan for Finding Peace in a Frantic World*[153] also is a terrific read with many helpful hints on how to balance our busy schedules and find our inner tranquility. I was especially drawn to the chapter asking when we stopped dancing because long ago I fell in love with Lee Ann Womack's song/poem entitled "I Hope You Dance."

Whether I'm listening to it being sung or reading the words, I have only to pause, close my eyes, and have a "self" moment of quiet reflection. It is truly a spiritual moment. Sometimes, I've only to read one line, and I transcend from inner turmoil to peace.

To appreciate the benefits of mindfulness, pause and feel the moment. Enjoy the sun on your face or the breeze tossing your hair. Ponder the beauty around you, the miracle of a robin's flight or a wren's chirp. Live the moment with curiosity and amazement. To do so brings spiritual healing and strength. Through prayer, Scripture reading, and/or mindfulness, we explore and experience inner serenity. What a gift! And in the doing, we rejuvenate our core, our heart.

Archway 1—Lessons Learned from the Lighthouse
Past—Present—Future

I have long since been intrigued with lighthouses. While in the past, they served our country and its many travelers from the shoals of disaster, they still today ring of hope and journey's mercies. From them I have gleaned some thoughts that may help those who suffer from

PTSD and those who care for them as they traverse their pathways through the darkness.

The lighthouse has an audacious past, a so-so present, but a hopeful future. And so do we. The lighthouse warned ships of hidden dangers along the shoreline and its effectiveness dates into antiquity when men would light fires on the tops of mountains to warn mariners of shallow and rocky beachfronts. While there may be somewhere in the neighborhood of a thousand lighthouses in the United States, they are not unique to this country; they are prevalent around the world. Michigan has some 150 lighthouses, indicative of our migration trends in the nineteenth century.

No one doubts the bravery experienced by our warriors on the Vietnam battlefields. Over the past forty-some years they have forged their way through the minefields of memory. Today they stand stouthearted—in some cases brazen, and in other cases defiant. What the future holds is only speculative, but I think these mighty men of valor will be unabashedly stalwarts of society. Their experiences in Vietnam, the drama thrust on them by a virulent society, and their journey through the quagmire of the Veterans Administration System, has already created new pathways for the veterans of today. Like a lighthouse, our warriors have been a beacon of light and will continue to be so.

Archway 2—Lessons Learned from the Lighthouse
Unique

No two lighthouses are alike, and no two warriors are alike; neither are their experiences on the battlefield. As I sat listening to the Vietnam veterans tell of their war experiences, I was impressed with the different recollections. Two warriors experiencing the same battle within a few feet of each other relate different views. One of the beauties of the Vietnam veterans' unit reunions has been the exchange of information. And it's amazingly healing.

I well remember how Dr. Johnson and Charlie Taylor filled in the blanks and reviewed the maps for Terry Gander and his friend, Ken Lancaster, who had no idea where they had been dropped geographically. Both had been wounded in a battle where they were not privy to the orders from those in headquarters. Simply obeying the commands given by their immediate field officers, they hopped onto a helicopter and jumped off at the landing zone.

Not only does each man's view of the war differ, but each man is unique. He deciphers his emotions and psychological response to the events distinctively. Therefore, we can assume the journey through their lives since Vietnam is unique. Each and every warrior has been molded and reshaped by his experiences throughout life, and most especially in combat. His and her individuality is a blessing.

Martin Luther King Jr. is credited to have said, "The ultimate measure of a man is not where he stands in the moments of comfort and convenience, but where he stands at times of challenge and controversy."[154] Our warriors have withstood the test and have excelled.

My purpose for thrashing through this concept is first and foremost to honor the individuality of each warrior, and second, to urge each warrior and their family members to strengthen their uniqueness. I pray each reader will also honor and develop their inward person. People leave imprints on our lives, and I for one am grateful that each of the imprints stamped upon my life is unrivaled and different from every other.

Archway 3—Lessons Learned from the Lighthouse
Purpose Driven

While every lighthouse is unique in their appearance and general overall makeup, they had one central purpose: beaming a light from the top of its tower to warn sailing crews of dangerous shorelines. Many lives, ships, and cargo would have been utterly and needlessly lost had the light been extinguished. Lighthouses had purpose and so do we. The question is, what is our purpose?

Somewhere along life's journey we hear about setting goals, most especially SMART goals, and B-HAG.

S – Specific

M – Measureable

A – Attainable

R – Realistic

T—Timely

B – Big

H – Hairy

A – Audacious

G – Goals

I recently heard a motivational speech using these concepts. It is my belief that many of us dream of bold and timely goals. I like to think of it as dreaming big dreams and then putting action into them. Flour is one ingredient in a cake, but it is not the cake. It takes a number of other ingredients to make it a delectable treat. So my message to all our readers is this: Dream with a purpose in mind and move forward. Ron Miriello is a prime example of someone who embraced his purpose. Years ago he set out to put the myths of Vietnam to rest by developing a PowerPoint presentation entitled "Vietnam—The Way It Was." He expounds eloquently in a variety of venues—colleges, state groups and organizations, and service clubs. His wife, Debbie, said, "Ron says doing this is therapy to him. It is his goal to educate the many who know little (or nothing) about what he calls the 'Forgotten War.'"

Dr. James Johnson is another who put purpose into action. Barbara said, "Jim's letters from Vietnam were very detailed as to the combat he was experiencing. But there were only facts—nothing as to the trauma. It was many, many years after the war before I realized the extent of the trauma these 'facts' had caused. It was when Jim began writing his first book *Combat Chaplain: A Thirty Year Vietnam Battle* that I began to learn of the trauma and how it impacted him."

In 2010, Jim published a second book, *Combat Trauma: A Personal Look at Long-Term Consequences*. Both books clearly fulfill a purpose from which we all find healing and strength. Jim's work is his purpose.

Not everyone wants to write books and make speeches, but everyone has purpose. I believe the most powerful purpose, which applies to all humanity, is to love others and to assist others when and where needed. Our purpose may be unique to us, but it typically affects others. Purpose resounds best when it harmonizes with or for the benefit of others. No one is a soloist; we are members of a choir. Together, we bring harmony and hope to all mankind.

But…you say.

What if…you say.

Again, I firmly believe we all have dreams and those dreams lend purpose to our lives and the lives of others. We can fulfill those dreams. Yes, distracters and distractions exist, but we do not have to relinquish our personal power to defeat. People, events, and things may bind us for a time, but we can choose to fulfill our dreams.

Two roadblocks that discourage us are past disappointments and past hurts. Others may be a lack of confidence or the lack of imagination. In John C. Maxwell's book *Own Your Dreams*, he says; "If you are unsure of what your dream might be, start preparing yourself to receive your dream by doing six things."[155] In summary they are:

1) Mental preparation: Read and study stuff that interest you.
2) Engage in activities that relate to your interest.
3) Visual preparation: Display pictures of people or things that inspire you.
4) Read about the people you admire. Try to meet them.
5) Be prepared physically to pursue your dream.
6) Seek God's help.

Golda Meir said; "Trust yourself. Create the kind of self that you will be happy to live with all of your life. Make the most of yourself by fanning the tiny, inner sparks of possibility into flames of achievement."[156]

Archway 4—Lessons Learned from the Lighthouse
Fresnel Lamps

The Fresnel lens was developed by French physicist Augustin-Jean Fresnel. By trimming away excess glass, Fresnell created a lighter lens. In most cases, these lenses had the ability to shine farther out to sea. Multifocal Fresnell lenses have been used in cameras and popular entertainment. Fresnel screens have been used as magnifiers for small CRT (cathode ray tube) monitors, and they are also used in aircraft carriers and naval air stations assisting in landing systems.[157]

Key here are two concepts—less material and potential for greater use and effectiveness. What started out as an improved lighting system for lighthouses has grown into a number of other inventions already in use. Can we assume there is more to come?

We may wonder how all of this applies to the spouses' response to their warriors' PTSD. Vietnam is a part of our past, indelibly written on the hearts and minds of the warriors who fought there. Can anything good come of that? Let us explore some ideas.

One of the most powerful effects coming out of the war has been the Brotherhood_which is a beacon meant to rescue those who suffer from horrendous memories of fighting and dying. I have seen veterans who come to reunions for the first time find their bearings. The camaraderie is palpable. Strong roots of understanding and caring begin to grow and then blossom. Most spouses have found that the effect carries their warrior through the up-and-down drama of life—the yo-yo times.

Reunions are not the only means of trimming away the excess burdens. Such may be found at the American Legion or the VFW. Vet Centers provide invaluable counseling and other resources. The real strength, however, lies in warrior to warrior. For the spouse, it's a lighter burden to carry; the shadows are less encompassing. As a spouse, we know we cannot cure PTSD, but we can care—care for our warriors, ourselves, and for other spouses. Jim Johnson likes to say, "It is more blessed to care than to cure."

One last question—what has this to do with aging?

Aging is like the yo-yo. We have up times and down times—both physically and psychologically. We strive to age wisely and healthily.

Archway 5—Lessons Learned from the Lighthouse
The Lighthouse Keeper

In the early days, a lighthouse keeper had three functions—one, to trim the wicks and feed the fuel resources; two, maintaining the lighthouse; and three, to rescue people from peril.

Sounds a lot like spousal responsibilities, doesn't it? Clean house, cook meals, run a taxi service, and be the chief purchasing agent and medical advisor. On some level, spouses hold the Geiger counter and constantly monitor the "radiation" levels of the family members' attitudes. On top of the normal routines, many spouses also work outside the home. Others are retired. I've come to the conclusion that success is generated in our own attitudes and responses to and toward our responsibilities. If we are a lighthouse keeper and stressed to the max, we are not working at optimum levels.

Rule number one—take care of ourselves first. If that means a day in the recliner with a good book, take it. Second rule—find humor. If for no other reason than to have a good laugh, check out gender differences. I love what one motivational speaker said: Men's brains are a collection of boxes and women's brains are like spaghetti. Men process one thing at a time; women multitask. A speech I heard recently talked about the differences in gestures—men have large movements, women tend to have close to the body movement. Find a bit of humor and enjoy healthy laughter. Don't forget to feed your spirit—good reading, gracious friendships, and a spiritual connection. In other words, keep your heart uncluttered from challenges that drag you down.

In Conclusion

Sophia Loren said, "There is a fountain of youth: it is your mind, your talents, the creativity you bring to your life and the lives of people you love. When you learn to tap this source, you will truly have defeated age."[158]

Good luck and God bless!

We can see and understand
Only a little about God now,
As if we are peering at his reflection in a poor mirror
But someday we are going to see him in his completeness,
Face to face.
Now all that I know is hazy and blurred,
But then I will see everything clearly, just as clearly
As God sees into my heart right now.
1 Corinthians 13:12

CHAPTER 18
Nightmares and Sleep Disorders

"In Vietnam, we were blindsided by ambushes, snipers, booby traps, rocket-propelled grenades, and mortars. Today, we are blindsided by nightmares, flashbacks, anger, depression, anxiety, guilt, and many other symptoms of our trauma."[159] (Dr. James Johnson)

"In Dave Schoenian's dreams, he is always being chased by the enemy and sometimes left behind, alone. His M-16 has no bullets. His dreams are brutal with lots of killing."[160]

Soon after getting out of the army in 1969, Roy Moseman began having nightmares. They were so bad that he dreaded going to sleep. He would intentionally get drunk nightly and pass out so he wouldn't have nightmares."[161]

When Charlie Taylor first arrived home from Vietnam, his nightmares were frequent and violent. He and his men were under fire and unable to move. He wanted to maneuver, but the mud was unyielding. As the years have passed, the nightmares have become fewer in number, and he is able to call in air support and artillery ground fire. Thus he feels mobile and more in control. The trauma, however, remains.

Janett, a close friend, shared this story about her father who served in World War II. He had nightmares all his life. Once while dreaming he was bailing out of a plane, he put his hand through the bedroom window and severed an artery.

Combat trauma is not unique to a specific war, but common to all. No fetters restrain it—without regard to the individual, the hour of the night, or the calendar day and year. Nightmares are realistic enactments of actual events or some combination of several wartime encounters.

Nightmares—The Devil's Playground

A nightmare is a frightening dream and an experience, situation, or object producing a feeling of anxiety or terror. Warriors who suffer with nightmares say they relive intense and vivid terror and emotions that closely resembles their combat experiences.

Charlie Taylor said, "The night before an operation I agonized about what I would encounter. During the encounter with the enemy, I would go into an adrenaline induced mode, doing what was required to do to keep myself and my men alive. After the fact, we all would sometimes laugh and joke about the ordeal. Laughter often relieves tension, but it only masks the raw emotion. When the laughter ceases, reality often sets in and often the tears begin to flow."

What appears to be a natural progression while they were in the war zone is really much more complicated over the long haul. Those experiences some forty-plus years ago play out later in a warrior's sleep and in some case throughout their waking hours as well. What we know from various studies is that in the face of danger the body kicks in a massive dose of adrenaline and the mind tapes the event much like a movie on a DVD. According to Wikipedia/Epinephrine/adrenaline, "adrenergic hormones can produce retrograde enhancement of long-term memory". In other words, when Charlie went into "adrenaline mode," his brain recorded the event and the emotions he experienced at that moment and it continually plays over and over and over. It doesn't go away and it doesn't reduce in intensity. If anything, the true fears and the imagined fears become one and the same. They often surface in nightmares.

Lynne Moseman said, "Roy never talked about any of the unpleasant aspects of being a nineteen-year-old soldier in a major combat zone. He would tell some funny stories about the guys he served with and different things they did to entertain themselves in the field. Although Roy suffered with nightmares the entire forty years of our marriage, he never shared them with me—until fifteen years into our marriage. He's never slept well and constantly continues to dream that he is back in Vietnam and can't leave the country because his paperwork isn't in order. He also dreams he's in a firefight and his rifle jams or he will run out of ammunition. After the war Roy became a heavy drinker. He 'self-medicated' because he hoped it would help him sleep. In spite of all this, he never missed a day of work because of his drinking, and he has never been violent."

"Terry has violent dreams and there is no doubt in my mind that he is fighting for his life," says Donna Gander. "I, in more times than not, am on the receiving end. He feels so bad when he wakes up. It's so hard for me to witness him relive the horrors of war in his dreams."

Metz's dreams are so bad that he and Barbara decided to buy a house with two master bedrooms—one on each end of the house—one for him and one for Barbara. Metz is kind and a gentleman in all sense of the word, but at night when the mind seeks rest, the past raises its head and roars.

Nightmares—Experts Say

Some experts say that nightmares are to the night what flashbacks are to the day. They are reincarnations of past events usually to some exaggerated degree. They sometimes create attitudes of despair, anxiety, and great sadness. In a generic sense, nightmares may contain unresolved issues that need to be addressed. For those suffering from PTSD, they are typically a reenactment of events where they felt extreme trauma. Most of the combat veterans I've spoken with feel high degrees of helplessness. Nightmares are usually long, intense, and reoccurring.

"Posttraumatic nightmares are repetitive and possess more memory intrusion of the traumatic event than ordinary nightmares. Their content consists of an exact replay of an actual scene or even from the disaster or traumatic event."[162] Not only are they repetitive, but they have minimal adaptive responses to the threats arising within the dream. They provoke anxiety. "Intolerable emotions and conflicts linked to the traumatic even continue to affect the individual's psyche, but are banned from consciousness so they can persist in nightmares."[163]

"Nightmares are 1 of 17 possible symptoms of PTSD. Nightmares are one of the most common of the 're-experiencing' symptoms of PTSD, seen in approximately 60 percent of individuals with PTSD."[164]

Nightmare Therapy

In *Healing War Trauma: A Handbook of Creative Approaches*, Raymond Monsour Scurfield and Katherine Theresa Platoni say that therapy consists of three steps. Step one prepares an individual suffering with traumatic nightmares to work through "psychoeducation about dysfunctional sleep, traumatic nightmares, and goals for resolving nightmares."[165] In other words, an individual is encouraged to self-educate, to learn something about dysfunctional sleep, sleep cycles, and levels of sleep.

Step two deals with the telling of the nightmare and the emotions connected with the nightmare. With the guidance of a counselor, the client describes their nightmare. Thoughts regarding the event are noted as are emotions. The therapist can record specific words or phrases which may produce a segue between the dream and unresolved issues. Scurfield and Platoni said, "A client is more likely to identify a traumatic memory once these are more apparent, and this allows the therapist to discuss the emotional impact of a traumatic event more openly."[166]

In step three an action plan is developed. This part creates a therapy regimen which may include "writing assignments, performing grief rituals, or other ideas which target unresolved issues in the dreamwork session."[167]

Also of interest from Scurfield's and Platoni's comments is the following: "clients often fail to identify nightmares (including those in which they see deceased people they have known) as indicative of unfinished or unresolved relationships."[168] This may indicate memories of guilt where the individual felt helpless and unable to influence the outcome of a traumatic event.

A similar treatment developed by Barry Krakow and his colleagues at the University of New Mexico treats nightmares with "Imagery

Rehearsal Therapy." "In brief, the treatment involves helping the clients change the endings of their nightmares, while they are awake, so that the ending is no longer upsetting."[169] It is classified as a cognitive-behavioral treatment and is similar to the treatment promoted by Scurfield and Platoni.

Of those men Dr. Johnson interviewed for his book *Combat Trauma: A Personal Look at Long-Term Consequences*, Ron Miriello comments on a similar technique that bridges his nightmares from trauma to a somewhat restfulness. It closely resembles step two above. "Dreaming of being back in Vietnam for Ron Miriello causes him to awaken in sweat. He has learned, however, to awaken himself and be assured that he is in the ease and comfort of home, not on a gun mount on a floating target on a muddy Mekong Delta waterway."[170]

Debbie Miriello said, "Ron has nightmares, but they just aren't noticeable to me."

Donna Gander said, "Terry has violent dreams. There is no doubt in my mind that he is fighting for his life."

Dr. Johnson said, "A continuing dream for me is of being with my men when a firefight begins and we are about to be overrun by the enemy. Being a chaplain, I never went into combat carrying a weapon. I saw my role to minister to my soldiers prior to and in the midst of combat. In the dream, I feel helpless and immobilized. The battle of Snoopy's Nose on September 15, 1967, is a dream that I have had probably over a hundred times. I see the boats on fire, the explosions all around, hear the small-arms fire hitting the sides of the boats, and see the blood-covered well deck of the navy ATC that wiped out one Company A, 3/60th Infantry's platoons with a B-40 rocket. I am trying to patch up the wounded, but I feel helpless in this dream as so many are wounded."[171]

"Jim's nightmares are prevalent. He awakens extremely fatigued," says Barbara Johnson.

This therapy for breaking the nightmare cycle may seem overly simplified, but it is far more than an A-B-C program and should be followed under the supervision of a qualified therapist. Is it worth the effort? Absolutely! Will talking about a nightmare be scary? I think that is a strong possibility. Could it be worth the risk? Most likely. Keep in mind that "Nightmare Therapy" is one way of addressing repetitious nighttime horror. Also keep in mind that "Action Plan Activities" vary and a knowledgeable, caring counselor should know what is best for the individual seeking beneficial results.

Fostering Sleep

Before we move on to why therapy is necessary for reducing nightmares, let us look at two suggestions given by Dr. Mark Goulston, MD and former assistant clinical professor of psychiatry at UCLA. First, he suggests the patient use "Image Rehearsal Therapy." Second, he suggests a technique called "Lucid Dreaming Treatment (LDT)."[172]

Image Rehearsal Therapy mirrors the "Nightmare Therapy" taught by Scurfield and Platoni and is much like stage 2. Goulston suggest you write down your nightmare and change the ending, then rehearse the new endings just before bedtime.

LDT is a technique that teaches you to gain a degree of control over your dreams while they are happening. "The treatment involves a range of techniques (for instance, dream recall, dream rehearsal, self-suggestion, and changes in sleeping schedules) that help you achieve lucidity—that is, the knowledge that you're dreaming—so that nightmares have less power over you."[173]

Dr. Goulston also suggests you rehearse your dream mentally in the daytime. When you reach the scary part, put your hands up as if you are stopping the motion and say, "This is a dream."[174]

Why Is Therapy Necessary?

Nightmares causing sleep deprivation can be subtle and deadly. Sleep deprivation affects the cognitive function of the brain. Needless to say, sleepiness may lead to unsafe driving or inefficient work habits. A report by Dr. Sheldon Sheps from Mayo Clinic said that lack of sleep may cause high blood pressure. "It's thought that sleep helps your blood regulate stress hormones and helps your nervous system remain healthy. Over time, a lack of sleep could hurt your body's ability to regulate stress hormones, leading to high blood pressure."[175]

In an article regarding lack of sleep by Timothy Morgenthaler, M.D., published by Mayo Clinic, the question of lack of sleep and sickness was addressed. Dr. Morgenthaler said. "During sleep, your immune system releases proteins called cytokines, some of which help promote sleep. Certain cytokines need to increase when you have an infection or inflammation, or when you're under stress. Sleep deprivation may decrease production of these protective cytokines."[176] He goes on to say that lack of sleep may increase the risk of obesity, diabetes, and cardiovascular disease.

NIGHTMARES—Spousal Response

Experiencing nightmares from a spousal point of view is often a situation of helplessness. It's pretty much a known fact that if a spouse chooses to awaken a warrior while he fights his way through a nightmare, she does so risking frightful responses. Rule of thumb—awaken a warrior very, very carefully.

Donna Gander says, "I, more times than not, am on the receiving end of Terry's bad dreams. He feels bad when he wakes up. It's so hard for me to witness him relive the horrors of war in his dreams."

Charlie Taylor cries out in his sleep. Some men talk in his sleep. Metz yells. Others toss about vigorously. The response may differ, but the geneses began in combat. The name of the war doesn't matter—World War II, Korea, Vietnam, Iraq, or Afghanistan. Nightmares are indicative of PTSD. And most combat veterans have some degree of post traumatic stress which may or may not be diagnosed as a "disorder."

Marianne said, "Forty-plus years after Bill served two tours, my husband still fights the war in his sleep. Sometimes it means he wakes up at 3 AM and just stares at the ceiling, and other times I hear him yell or hear him panting as if running in fear. In the early days, I dare not touch him during those times because he would swing wildly in the air. Now I am able to just lightly stroke his arm or back and tell him that I am there and that everything is okay. Still, sometimes he jerks away until he wakes up and realizes it was just a dream. Then he calms down but usually has trouble falling back asleep.

"Worse than the night dreams, though, are the days when I (Marianne) sense his anxiety is building. It is then that I walk on eggshells for fear of prompting an angry response. I always see the angst build before he does. He acknowledges this and has worked extremely hard to deal with it without affecting me, but still, I feel it and dread knowing that we will be going through a rough spell. I can only describe it as feeling like watching a switch being thrown in his brain and seeing a different person come out—one who lashes out at me with hurtful and cutting words. We have survived this type of reaction together. I understand how PTSD works."

Archway—1

It is important for you, the spouse of a warrior who suffers from nightmares, to get sufficient sleep. Take care of yourself. Here are a few suggestions from the Mayo Clinic:

1) Stick to a sleep schedule. Go to bed at a set time regardless of the day of the week or the season of the year. Do whatever it takes to be relaxed when you hit the sack. For me (Diana) that is "light" reading. Needless to say, I read a lot of "heavy" material during the day as I'm working, but in the evening I do something for fun. I like "easy" crossword puzzles and "easy" Sudoku. In years past, I read a lot of novels, especially romances. When I worked as a certified financial planner, I spent many hours reading tax material, stock options, clients' files and the like. When I got home from the office the last thing I wanted just before bedtime was to read something educational. I wanted something to make my mind relax.

2) Pay attention to what you eat and drink. Most would agree that caffeine of any sort is a stimulant and not a sleep-aid. Avoid them. Over or under eating should be avoided also. If you like the taste of warm milk, go for it.

3) Create an atmosphere that is conducive to sleep. Not too hot or cold and preferably dark and quiet. If you are like most couples, someone is usually hot and someone is chilled and you've learned to compensate for this difference.

On a different note, what does one do if their partner snores? A few years ago, I did a sleep test and found that I had sleep apnea. Charlie sleeps a lot better since I've been using my C-Pap. If someone you know snores, I recommend you have a sleep study. Snoring is a sign of improper breathing and may signal a need for opening the nasal passages which allows for sufficient oxygen to reach the lungs, blood, and vital organs of the body.

It is not uncommon for combat veterans to be diagnosed with sleep apnea. It is common for combat veterans to not breathe when under stress.[177] Testing for sleep disorders such as sleep apnea may help both partners.

4) Regular physical activity is conducive to better sleep. The best time for exercise is early in the day.

Archway—2

What can we do to help our spouses overcome the trauma of nightmares? It may take a series of experiments and exercises. My immediate thoughts were if the five suggestions listed above work for us, and for most people, why not try them as they are or with a suitable makeover, on our spouses. A lot can be said for regular exercise and routines such as going to bed at a regular time.

In *Operators Manual for Combat PTSD*, Ashley B. Hart II, Ph.D. stresses the importance of deep breathing relaxation techniques prior to sleep. This technique may require some practice. He also suggests that medications, both natural and pharmaceutical, may be useful and necessary.[178]

Therapists recommend the warrior talk through and journal about the nightmares. Perhaps one way to help would be to encourage dialogue and listen to their stories. Then help them imagine a workable ending—an ending that would resolve or lessen the terror.

Most men won't read romance, but light reading before bedtime is a viable option. One of my favorite books is written by Andy Andrews titled *The Butterfly Effect: How Your Life Matters*. It's a small book—109 pages. Mr. Andrews says, "Every single thing you do matters. You have been created as one of a kind. You have been created in order to make difference. You have within you the power to change the world."[179] I recommend you go to his website: www.simpletruths.com. Explore the plethora of books similar to this one—light, inspirational reading. Quotes by famous people may change the direction of our thinking and encourage us to persevere. Biographies of famous people or not-so-famous people tend to encourage us to raise our expectations of ourselves.

One of my favorite biographies is the story of Fanny Crosby who lived ninety-five years, most of those years during the nineteenth century. Blinded when only a few months old through a medical mishap, she wrote over 8000 hymns and a number of other songs. She also taught school and lobbied Congress for the education of the blind. Her story and the stories of many others from today and yesteryears can be found on Wikipedia and in books. Check out Amazon.

Archway—3

Meditation, sometimes referred to as "mindfulness," can be a positive way to reduce stress and encourage relaxation. For me (Diana), meditation is synonymous with scripture recitation and prayer. For others it may be the recitation of poetry or a listing of things to be grateful for. Some people use this time to empty their minds, but I believe it is more beneficial to pursue prosperity-of-thought—fill your mind and heart with worthwhile, happy thoughts.

I have long been a restless sleeper and found it difficult to fall asleep. Years ago I discovered what I call thought-control. I simply use the alphabet to focus my thoughts. I might sing a song that starts with A and continue to sing my way through the alphabet—all in my head, of course. Rarely do I get to "Z". If I get distracted, I quote scriptures beginning with "A" and work my way through the letters. Sometimes I think of people to pray for using the alphabet. I suggest a grateful list using the letters from A to Z. The opportunities are endless. Be creative.

Steven M. Southwick, MD, and Dennis S. Charney, MD, in their book entitled; *Resilience: The Science of Mastering Life's Greatest Challenges*, say, "Many meditative traditions teach that such efforts can increase personal freedom, which grows out of an enlarged capacity to modify thoughts and feelings, as well as change behaviors."[180]

IN CONCLUSION

Some have said the more severe the trauma, the more apt that individual will suffer from nightmares. Seems like a reasonable conclusion, but let's not give up hope. More and more information is coming to light that may help the sufferer. As our warriors become more involved in their healing of PTSD, the more promise we have that the nightmares can be modified. When the warrior comes to the realization that he or she has done their best in the field, the greater the possibility of them coming to grips with these nighttime intrusive events. The possibilities lead me to hope for better and better results. We are not looking for a pie-in-the-sky panacea, but for true and lasting healing.

THE SOLDIER IN MY BEDROOM

The soldier in my bedroom once was a boy,
Never knew by joining one day he would deploy
Dropped by helicopter in a place so far from home,
Age and lost security he felt so all alone.

Wading through the mud dodging bullets left and right,
Whose idea was it to ever start this fight?
Hunger approaches finding food by way of can,
Why couldn't he be another place than Vietnam?

Lying on the ground fighting for his life,
Thinking of his hometown where he left his wife.
Will she wait for him being gone so long?
Now was not the time to think he needed to be strong.

Suddenly he hears a cry his best friends hit,
Holding each other together there they sit.
His clothes turn red his best friends dead,
The words I love you can't be said.

He's in the air his thoughts repeat,
The airplane lands his wife he'll meet.
Clinging together like vines on a wall,
Home from the war he gave his all.

The soldier in my bedroom lies with me each night,
Tossing and turning wishing for the light.
Sleep comes not often and dreams interrupt,
Morning persuades exhaustion with the need to get up.

Daylight brings protection from the shadows of the dark,
The sound of planes or thunder always starts a spark.
Remembering the gunfire and having hit the ground,
The screaming in the background gives off an eerie sound.

There is no vacation from the memories in his mind,
He prays for amnesia to take the past that bind.
The battlefield crawls in his thoughts he'll least expect,
Alerted to the noises he never will forget.

Again tonight the soldiers will pierce in his dreams,
Haunting hours of nightfall never ending it seems.
There may come a time when his memories will fade,
Perhaps now at peace his body is laid.

June Mare Carolus

There are three things that remain—
faith, hope, and love—
and the greatest of these is love.
1 Corinthians 13:13

Chapter 19
Vietnam—Then and Now

Unprecedented shelling ripped through the morning dawn as Charlie shot and killed four men. He took aim at another, but soon realized this man was in chains. He aimed at another and discovered a woman whose face and name he knew. As a condolence for this near accident, he gave her a weird look. Then he awakened, knowing it was all a nightmare, another nightmare, one of many that rebirthed events for his time in Vietnam four decades prior. Like most who served in that combat, his war experiences have been deeply etched into his memory never to be forgotten—altered at times, tweaked in some bizarre way, but with every sensory factor of the body, tangible night and day.

Ask any combat veteran who served in Vietnam when he was there. More often than not, he will tell you last night. The war lives on. What was then is now. The muck and mire of yesterday is ever present today. Like incoming and outgoing fire, it comes and goes. In this chapter, I want to look at the then-and-now effects on the mind and heart of the warriors and their families.

No One Left Behind

Warriors would risk life and limb to save a Brother on the battlefield. No one was left behind. What was true in the war zone is now true on the home front. Most combat veterans, spouses or significant others, and family members have done their best to keep the warrior and the family unit intact, even as they battle the destructive effects of PTSD.

Today while the past haunts many of our brave warriors, it also has contributed to the strongest bond of Brotherhood one could have ever imagined. From all walks of life, warriors find common ground at our unit reunions. Some of the darkest days of their lives have contributed a welcomed bond of love and appreciation for one another. When these warriors come together—and they do, from all over the United States—they support each other with respect and gratitude. They laugh. They cry. Past rank has no meaning. They are Brothers whose ties are as strong—and in some cases stronger—than genetic siblings. Not a spouse I know would disagree.

Donna Gander says, "Terry is a whole new man for a few weeks, sometimes months, after we return from the reunions. He is grateful to be able to see the Brothers that can make it. They talk or email each other throughout the year. For Terry to see them, hug them, talk to them makes a big difference. At the reunions he is finally able to talk about the battles and the scars they left—not only his, but his Brothers as well. The 'Warrior Pack' is a tight group of brave men and they are— and always will be—there for each other and their spouses."

Dr. Jim Johnson attended his first reunion because Barbara—who has always been tremendously supportive—insisted he go. Jim brings a spirit of healing with him. Both warriors and wives appreciate and benefit from his compassion and wit.

Marianne said her husband, Bill, and many of his friends prefer to meet one-on-one. I agree. It's not about the numbers around the table, but the love and understanding that binds our warriors together. The Brotherhood—a fortress like nothing else.

On the other hand, JoAnn Moore said, "I can't say enough good about reunions. I don't know where we would be today if Guy hadn't gone to a reunion the first time John Sperry invited him. John led us to the first reunion in 2005 where Guy got to see John Ianucci for the first time in thirty-plus years, along with Lieutenant Charles Howe, Denny McDougal, David Graves, and others. I was awestruck at how they treated Guy and the respect they had for him. It made me feel good about who he was and is.

"Barbara Ianucci took me (JoAnn) under her wing at that first reunion. I never felt out of place. I can't imagine life without the reunions. The wives are the best! We may see them once a year or once every other year, but when we are all together, it's like no time has passed since the last time we saw each other."

Indeed, the bond between the wives has grown and bloomed with every reunion. No woman has been left behind. As Donna said, "I personally feel elated to see everyone—the warriors, wives, and significant others, and sometimes the sons and daughters. The ladies are all wonderful, and over the years, we have become a tight group as well."

We rally to the call for help from other spouses, significant others, and family members. No one is left behind—not the warriors and not the family members.

As Charlie and I reflected on the reunions we attended this year, we concluded that the Vietnam combat veterans have finally come into their own. They are stepping out and being counted—not just at the reunions, but everywhere. We see stickers on cars, embroidered hats and shirts, and other various proclamations. It seems apparent that they no longer care what Joe Blow on the street thinks. They are comfortable in their skin. They are proud of their service to our country. Their confidence does not depend on community acceptance. They hold their heads high and their shoulders pulled back with pride. Hallelujah!

Gear-Up

Returning to base camp was only a temporary reprieve from action. It was time to clean their weapons, dry out their feet, and get ready for the next call to saddle up. I noticed that in today's military, the term is often "Kit-Up." That means they and their equipment must be ready for whatever and wherever they are called up for duty. I use the term "Gear-Up" here to make the point that our warriors and their spouses are ready for action—today, tomorrow, the next day, or whenever duty beckons. This duty may be as little as a friendly hello, thank you for your service, or as complicated as taking a veteran to the VA or the Vet Center or guiding them through the quagmire of the "system." Our warriors and their spouses know the ropes and willingly and graciously walk another veteran through the maze or buy them lunch. They are ready and prepared.

As far as the world is concerned, the war in Vietnam ended with the signing of the Paris Peace Accord; however, such is not the case for many of the Vietnam combat veterans. As mentioned earlier, for them the war was last night. They have not forgotten the horrors of war, neither have they forgotten the dismal reception they received when they returned from the war zone, but that doesn't stop them from making a difference in their world today. The same holds true for the spouses and family members. These men and their spouses are making a difference in the lives of family members and neighbors in their communities and in their states.

Mary Galde said, "At work, I'm constantly volunteering to help with this committee or that—community clean-up, United Way, Harvest Food Bank, etc. I have an emotional reaction whenever I see a homeless vet holding up a sign; it always makes me tear up. I know the consensus around the country is that the homeless should pick themselves up and get a job, but when I see some of them—especially the older ones—all bent over, dirty and sad, it breaks my heart. I will never pass them by without some small monetary contribution. In my head I think, "There but for the grace of God could be Dan or my son, Don."

This came from Terry and Barbe Balfe:

"When we go to Atlantic City, we always stop and talk to the street people who most often are Vietnam vets. We speak to them so often that not only do we know their names, but they also know ours. There are two in particular we love to see—Fanny, a gospel singer, and Stanley the Vietnam vet.

"Terry and Stanley have this thing going now that when we go over to him Terry asks him if he remembers Terry's name. The first time, even though Stanley remembered us, he forgot Terry's name. He couldn't. Terry gave him ten dollars and promised more, especially if he remembered Terry's name. The next time which may have been a year or so later, Stanley remembered his name. Not only that, but he extended his hand in greeting. "This guy has a smile that makes you melt with compassion. He and Terry had a good long talk about benefits a few years back and Terry encouraged him not to give up. When we saw him next, he was so excited to show us his disability check which he had just picked it up from the post office. He was overwhelmingly grateful for Terry's help and encouragement.

"Some people look at us like we're crazy talking and laughing with these people, but we don't care. We consider them our Atlantic City friends. Stanley says he doesn't consider us as just a handout but his friends as well. "Terry always talks to veterans when he sees them. The other day at the mall Terry spoke to a man who was walking his grandbaby around in the stroller. He joined us while we were having lunch. That would not have happened a few years ago. Terry sees it as one vet helping another.

We [Charlie and Diana] had a similar situation happen at the airport. I had been talking to my seatmate about Dan Galde and the Son Tay raid. When I exited the plane, a man who was sitting in front of me and who had been eavesdropping, challenged me about those who *think* they know someone who were part of that famous raid. I had barely reached the terminal from the causeway when he was in my face. I held my ground, but only after an exchange on the phone with Dan did he change his mind. (I have to inject at this point that I can be a bit feisty when I need to defend our warriors—these men whom I love and appreciate.) This gentleman who happened to be a veteran, but one who had never seen combat, bought our lunch. He also thanked Charlie for his service. An interesting turnaround for us. We often speak to the military people we encounter in our journeys, and like others we "secretly" buy meals for them.

Debbie Miriello said, "Ron drives people to their doctor's appointments, often out of town. When he sees a WW II veteran at a restaurant, he usually tells their waitress to bring him the bill (in secret) and to simply say "Thank you for being part of the world's greatest generation. It was an honor to pay for your meal."

"When a neighbor happened to say, 'I have always wanted to see the Grand Canyon, but it looks like it will never happen,' Ron asked why. The response was—'I'm losing my sight, can't drive, and won't be able to see it well enough to appreciate it soon anyway.' Ron's immediate response was, 'If you really want to take that trip, let's do it.' Soon after that night, we [Ron and Debbie] traveled with our neighbors across the country. We did Old Route 66, the Grand Canyon, Las Vegas, and much more. We traveled over fifty-two hundred miles and no one drove but Ron. I think that gesture gave Ron more pleasure than the trip itself."

Jim Carolus runs a weekly Bingo game as a fundraiser for the American Legion, just one of several ways this organization meets the needs of local military families. They help veterans with food, clothes, utility expenses and rent, and home and auto repairs. They also contact military "Family Support" sections of deployed units and assist the wives and families with the many needs—auto/home, financial aid, and more. Jim said, "We feel that our deployed military have enough to concern themselves with and worry about. They don't need to worry about their families being taken care of while they are away."

At the nearby Air National Guard Base, Jim's group is in contact with their family support organization—the Dependency Indemnity Compensation (DIC). They've learned that these families are also in need of financial help and they meet this need. They have applied for and received monies from "tobacco grants." This is a tremendous boost for meeting the needs of military families.

Dr. Jim Johnson has many unique opportunities to come alongside war-worn veterans. Because of his published works and his position as chaplain, Jim has been invited to interact with Vietnam veterans who suffer from PTSD and are on death row in Raleigh, North Carolina. On one such occasion he had the opportunity to pin the Purple Heart on an imprisoned veteran who is on death row. In 2005, Jim was invited by the warden of the infamous San Quentin State Prison in California to spend a few days with the then thirty-one Vietnam vets incarcerated there.

Jim is in contact with several hundred combat veterans. Almost daily, he is contacted by one or more vets, some he has never known before. He has assisted probably twenty or thirty with ideas of how they can enhance their paperwork for VA claims, especially for PTSD. Many have successfully filed their claims and received benefits.

Rich (a member of the 5/60) and Geraldine Guevara of Long Island, New York, help several military entities with financial support, and Barbara and Daniel Cannode are extremely involved with the Military Order of the Purple Heart. Barbara previously served as president of the Ladies Auxiliary. In the previous chapter, we spoke of Project Healing Waters, a project which is very meaningful to Dave Schoenian. He encourages veterans to participate, often putting their needs ahead of his own—once a platoon sergeant, always a platoon sergeant. Way to go, Dave! And Ken Costich actively promotes the benefits of Operation Wolfhounds 4-Vets (information in previous chapter). The needs seem endless, but our warriors and their spouses are stepping forward—no man or woman is left behind. We have geared-up and are battle ready.

Mary Galde said, "Both Dan and I find ourselves a little too busy sometimes—doing projects or helping someone else, either physically or financially—and many times it takes away from things we need to do for ourselves, or money we should be saving for the future. But I don't think I'd want it any other way. When it all rolls around, family and friends are the most precious things in life so nurturing and caring for them is number one."

As previously noted, on a more formal basis, Ron Miriello takes a professional PowerPoint presentation entitled "Vietnam—The Way It Was" to colleges, state groups, service clubs, and the like. He has done much to debunk the myths about the Vietnam War.

Dr. Jim Johnson has also given countless speeches to many groups about PTSD. Invariably, at the conclusion, many want to talk more and some have followed up with him in the days and weeks following.

Our Vietnam warriors and their spouses are geared-up and ready for service on many fronts. But much is yet to be done for our Vietnam veterans and much work lies ahead with our current veterans.

Walking Point—Reaching Out

On infantry patrols, someone had to be the point man who walks ahead of the rest of the infantrymen. How far ahead that man walked depended on the terrain and the number of men in the unit. In open ground, the distance will be considerably greater than when in the jungle, or in the case of crossing a stream, that distance was much shorter. Whatever the distance, walking point is nothing short of strolling into hell.

Most of our warriors would say that the trauma of war is always a second away. Terry Balfe said, "Vietnam is in my brain every day. Sometimes it's good and I wish I could be there right now—maybe to do things differently. Then there are days when it drives me crazy. My attitude has changed mostly for the positive."

Mary Galde said, "Dan has gone through his many, many years of disappointment, confusion, shame, and sadness. But now he's beginning to come out of the funk and into the light. He is finally getting the counseling he needed for so long where he's meeting others 'just like him.' Sharing stories with those who understand has helped a lot. He's beginning to feel pride again in his time as a pararescueman.

Barbe Balfe has seen a real change of attitudes toward the Vietnam veterans. She said, "Not only are Vietnam veterans approaching Terry and talking, sometimes in great lengths, but now children of vets are stopping him and wishing to share their father's experiences with him. That's amazing."

Sally C said of her husband, "It is only recently that he has become proud of his service and interested in the history of the war. He had been spit on and booed when he came home."

I recently spoke to a WWII veteran who proudly rattled off the battles he had been in. His memory was sharp and his bearing was one of pride. He had every right to wax eloquently about his service. I felt privileged to hear his candor. I believe the day is coming when our Vietnam veterans will be held in high esteem—or maybe it is already here. Our Vietnam veterans have had a tough road, but they are now receiving the praise they deserve.

Today, many of our warriors have navigated the halls of the VA and the Vet Centers seeking help for their PTSD. It's not been an easy journey. We could write a book on delays, lost files, and heaven knows what else. Every roadblock brought frustration and anger, and many a spouse has suffered right along with their warriors. But having blazed a few pathways, these men-on-point have taken many of the younger vets under their wings and guided them through the maze.

DD-214

When a man or woman leaves the military, he or she is issued a DD Form 214 which tells all the important details of their time of service, awards and medals, promotions, combat service or overseas service, Military Occupational Specialty identifiers, and record of training and schools completed. It is an extremely important document for those who have served in the military and for their families.

I use this term here as an analogy. While our warriors, like all servicemen and women, receive a DD Form 214 when they exit the military, we know their service did not leave them so easily. This important document gave them leave from their duties, but not from their memories.

So where's the analogy? The DD Form 214 is a doorway to start a new life. Good, bad, or indifferent, it is a new beginning. We are at the close of this book, and at the beginning of a new opportunity. Most who have contributed to this book—the warriors, the spouses, and the children—have migrated the turbulent waters of PTSD. Let it be said and understood that tomorrow is a new day, a new beginning.

Our memories are indelibly written on our brains and our hearts, but we have garnered wisdom and hope along the way. We candidly shared our experiences and wisdom of our troubling pasts from our hearts and our heads. We have endeavored to reach out to the many families who have walked or sailed similar pathways and waterways. We primarily represent the Vietnam era, but war is war. Trauma is trauma. We have walked point because we won't leave any man or woman behind. We stand ready—geared up—to walk with you who are presently walking where we once were some forty-plus years ago.

Archway 1—Know Your Rights and Privileges

The DD Form 214 is generally required by funeral directors in order to prove eligibility for interment in a VA cemetery and/or obtaining a grave marker and/or provide military honors. Such honors include the eligible veteran to receive a military funeral honors ceremony which includes the folding and presentation of the U.S. burial flag and the sounding of "Taps" at no cost to the family.

Check out http://usgovinfo.about.com/od/resourcesforveterans/a/dd214.htm. If someone you know doesn't have their DD-214, this website will lead them in the right direction for obtaining a new one. There are also other "usgov" sites that may be useful and/or informative. It never hurts to do an online search.

On a lighter note, I discovered that some cruise lines even offer an onboard spending amount for veterans, but you need the DD Form 214 to prove it. Makes me wonder what else is out there.

Most VAs and Vet Centers have literature which will clarify their services. They are there to help you. If you need an experienced veteran to guide you, one can be found. Also check out the American Legion and the Veterans of Foreign Wars. If you are the recipient of a Purple Heart, seek out a local unit of the Military Order of the Purple Heart and/or the Ladies Auxiliary of the Military Order of the Purple Heart. There may be an arm of these organizations in your community or in a nearby community.

Archway 2—Validation

I have spoken with a number of veterans and veterans' spouses. With the exception of very few, I have found that what most warriors want and need is acceptance. Self-doubt and guilt often override their value of themselves and their war experiences. These are brave men who were once young, valiant, and innocent boys. They fulfilled their duties as warriors. They fought a war because they were honorable. Our respect validates them and their service.

One key element in a good marriage *is* validation, especially in a marriage where one partner suffers from PTSD. For those who live with a warrior who suffers from PTSD, we recognize that conversation about the war is probably not going to happen. They may not tell you what happened to them day after day in Vietnam. However, our quiet acceptance of them as a person validates them. When we validate them, they are able to validate themselves and their spouses. Validation builds trust.

Earlier in this book we talked about how our Vietnam veterans have become more visible. They are wearing ball caps with "Vietnam Veteran" or something similar across the front and other times they wear T-shirts with something about Vietnam. In doing so, they proudly announce their service to this country in that conflict. Because of this new visibility, many of the vets engage another vet in conversation: When were you there? Where did you serve? and so on.

Terry and Barbe Balfe had a delightful exchange with a couple in Atlantic City who they thanked for their service. Barbe said, "When I thanked her, they both were stunned. Then he turned toward his spouse and thanked her for 'putting up with him.' Imagine," said Barbe, "all these years and they had never thought about it as fighting a battle alongside him." That's validation!

Such is also happening within the family. Ty, the son of a Vietnam veteran, attended the Mobile Riverine Force Reunion in 2013 where he accepted the Gold Medal in memory of his late father. Our son, Sam, is assistant historian for the 5th Battalion 60 Infantry Regiment reunion members. Both of our sons have been to the reunions, along with more and more of veterans' adult children and grandchildren who are attending reunions. This is validation. Recognizing the veterans and their service in Vietnam greatly enhances their appreciation of themselves and honors their service in the military.

In Conclusion

In this book, we have attempted to tell the spouses' stories—what it is like to live with a Vietnam combat veteran. Using Dr. Johnson's book *Combat Trauma: A Personal Look at Long-Term Consequences* as our platform, we have endeavored to tell what we did in order to survive our warriors' trauma. We've been candid. Sometimes life was tumultuous. Sometimes we, the spouses and children, suffered right along with our combat warriors. Other times we were able to smooth the roadways and calm the storms. In many cases, we stayed the course, although sometimes that was not possible. It is our hope and prayer that our experiences will give you insight and the courage to face your trauma and that of your spouse.

We've all come a long ways from the early days after the war. Name calling, ridicule, and antiwar marches are for the most part a thing of the past. Our warriors, their spouses, and families are walking tall. Now we have moved through our own trauma and have helped others. We endeavor to reach out to other veterans and their families regardless of the war. We want no one to be left behind.

Courage does not always roar.
Sometimes it is a quiet voice at the end of the
day, saying...*I will try again tomorrow.*
—Mary Anne Radmacher

THE END

ENDNOTES
Introduction

1 Johnson, James D. *Combat Trauma: A Personal Look at Long-Term Consequences* (Lanham, MD: Rowman & Littlefield Publishers, Inc., 2010), pp. 173-74.

2 Ibid., p. 174.

3 Alley, Lee with Stevenson, Wade. *Back from War: Finding Hope and Understanding in Life after Combat* (Exceptional Publishers, 2007),

4 Johnson, p. 8.

5 Ibid., p. 9.

6 Ibid.

7 Ibid.; Page 10.

8 Ibid.; Page 10.

Chapter 2

9 Burkett, B.G., and Whitley, Glenna. *Stolen Valor: How the Vietnam Generation Was Robbed of its Heroes and its History* (Dallas, TX: Verity Press Publishing, 1998),.

10 Johnson, *Combat Trauma* p. 149.

11 Ibid., p. 150.

12 Reed, Allen. "Vets Respond to Court Overturning Stolen Valor Law. Associated Press, July 02, 2012.

13 Johnson, *Combat Trauma*. p. 41.

14 Ibid.

15 Ron Minello, 2012, www.vietnamriverrat.com.

16 History.Com: Statistics about the Vietnam War; http://www.vhfcn.org/stat.html

17 History.com: Statistics about the Vietnam War; http:// www.vhfcn.org/stat.html;

18 www.vietnamriverrat.com; Ron Miriello; © 2012.

19 Ibid.

20 Ibid.

21 Ann Coulter. *Treason: Liberal Treachery from the Cold War to the War on Terrorism* Crown Forum) 2003; p. 131.

22 History.Com: Statistics about the Vietnam War; http://www.vhfcn.org/stat.html

23 Ibid.

24 "Opposition to the U.S. involvement in the Vietnam War"; Wikipedia.

25 "Draft Evasion"; Wikipedia.

26 *Webster's New Explorer College Dictionary, New Edition*; Created in co-operation with the editors of Merriam-Webster; Springfield, MA, 2007.

Chapter 3

27 History.com: Statistics about the Vietnam War; www.vhfcn.org/stat.html

28 *Combat Trauma: A Personal Look at Long-Term Consequences*; Dr. James D. Johnson; © 2010; Page 105.

Chapter 4

29 Ibid., p. 107.

30 Ibid., p. 108.

31 *History.com: Statistics about the Vietnam War*; http://www.vhfen.org/stat.html.

Chapter 5

32 *Combat Trauma: A Personal Look at Long-Term Consequences*; Dr. James D. Johnson; ©2010; Page 169.

33 Ibid; Page 170.

34 James D. Johnson. *Combat Trauma: A Personal Look at Long-Term Consequences*; Rowman and Littlefield Publishers, Inc., Lanham, Maryland 20706; © 2010; 101.

Chapter 6

35 Ibid; 102

36 Ibid. Page 105.

37 Glenn R. Schiraldi, Ph.D.; The Post-T SD Sourcebook: A Guide to Healing, Recovery, and Growth; McGraw Hill, New York; © 2009; Page 194.

38 Ibid; Page 249.

39 Ibid. Page 128

40 Ibid. Page 128

41 *USA Today*; "Study suggests feelings of guilt are a top PTSD cause"; Friday, November 25, 2011.

42 *Combat Trauma: A Personal Look at Long-Term Consequences*; Dr. James D. Johnson; © 2010; Page 102.

43 *Combat Trauma: A Personal Look at Long-Term Consequences*; Dr. James D. Johnson; © 2010; Page 104.

44 Ibid. Page 102.

45 Lee Alley; *After the War: Finding Hope and Understanding in Life After Combat*; Exceptional Pub; © 2007.

46 *Combat Trauma: A Personal Look at Long-Term Consequences*; Dr. James D. Johnson; © 2010; Page 99.

47 Integrity Notes: www.integritnotes.com; DaySpring Cards

48 Charles W. Hoge, MD, Colonel, U.S. Army (Ret.); *One is Once a Warrior, Always a Warrior: Navigating the Transition from Combat to Home*; © 2010; Page 262.

Chapter 7

49 Dr. James Johnson; *Combat Trauma: A Personal Look at Long-Term Consequences*; © 2010; Page 83

Chapter 8

50 *Combat Trauma: A Personal Look at Long-Term Consequences*; Dr. James D. Johnson; © 2010; Page 83.

51 *Webster's New World College Dictionary*; ©1996

52 *Combat Stress Injury: Theory, Research, and Management*; Edited by Charles R. Figley and William P. Nash; ©2007; Page 25.

53 Statistics about the Vietnam War; http://www.vhfcn.org/stat.html

54 *Combat Trauma; A Personal Look at Long-Term Consequences*; Dr. James Johnson; © 2010; Page 84.

55 *Combat Trauma: A Personal Look at Long-Term Consequences*; Dr. James D. Johnson; © 2010; Page 83.

56 Ibid.; Page 83.

57 Dr. James Johnson; *Combat Trauma: A Personal Look at Long-Term Consequences*; © 2010; Page 138.

Chapter 9

58 Ibid., p. 139.

59 Ibid.

60 Ibid., p. 138.

61 Ibid., p. 141.

62 *Once a Warrior—Always a Warrior, Navigating the Transition from Combat to Home, Including Combat Stress, PTSD, and TBI*; Charles W. Hoge, MD, Colonel, U.S. Army (Ret.); ©2010; Page 136-143.

63 Charles W. Hoge, MD, Colonel, U.S. Army (Ret.);.; Page 136.

64 Charles W. Hoge, MD, Colonel, U.S. Army (Ret.); Page 137.

65 Robert J. Morgan; *Nelson's Complete Book of Stories, Illustrations, and Quotes: The Ultimate Contemporary Resource for Speakers*; "Memorized Scripture at the Hanoi Hilton"; ©2000; Page 57-59

66 Htty://www.brainyquote.com

67 *Webster's New World College Dictionary*; © 1996.

Chapter 10

68 Dr. James Johnson; *Combat Trauma: A Personal Look at Long-Term Consequences*; © 2010; Page 35.

69 Ibid; Page 105.

70 Lori S. Rubenstein; *Forgiveness: Heal your past and find the peace you deserve*: Sacred Life Publishers; 2012; Page 22-23.

71 Ibid., p. 59.

72 Mayo Clinic Staff: *Forgiveness: Letting Go of Grudges and Bitterness.*

73 Ibid.

74 Glenn R. Schiraldi, Ph.D.; *The Post-Traumatic Stress Disorder Sourcebook: A Guide to Healing Recovery, and Growth;* Second Edition; © 2009; Page 308.

75 John C. Maxwell; Encouragement Changes Everything; ©2008; Page 20.

Chapter 11

76 Mark Epstein; Published on *Psychology Today* (http://www.psychologytoday.com) "Opening Up to Happiness".

77 Jonathan Shay, M.D., Ph.D., *Achilles in Vietnam: Combat Trauma and the Undoing of Character* (City, state of publication: name of publisher, 1994), p. 179.

Chapter 12

78 Andy Robertson; *The Bunny Platoon History 1968-1969;* © August 15, 2011, pp. 3-10.

79 Ibid.

80 Dr. James Johnson, *Combat Trauma: A Personal Look at Long-Term Consequences* (New York: Rowman and Littlefield Publishers, Inc., 2010), p. 80.

81 Ibid, p. 81.

82 Shay, *Achilles in Vietnam,* p. 178.

83 Ibid.,, p. 179.

84 Johnson, *Combat Trauma,* p. 172.

85 Ibid. Page 172.

86 Laurie B. Slone, PhD and Matthew J. Priedman, MD, PhD, *After the War Zone: A Practical Guide for Returning Troops and Their Families* (city, state: publisher, 2008), p. 173.

87 Johnson, p. 80.

88 Keith Armstrong, L.C.S.W./Susanne Best, Ph.D/ Paul Domenici, Ph.D.; *Courage After Fire: Coping Strategies for Troops Returning from Iraq and Afghanistan and Their Families* (city, state: publisher, 2006), p. 29.

89 Mayo Clinic staff; http://www.mayoclinic.com/health/positive-thinking/SR00009.

90 Ken Olsen; *The American Legion: The magazine for a strong America;* October 2012, pp. 44-50.

91 Andy Andrews; *Mastering the Seven Decisions that Determine Personal Success* (city, state: publisher, 2008), p. 56.

92 Ibid., p. 30.

93 *Orlando Sentinel,* 9 October 2012, page number?

94 Mitch Golant, Ph.D., and Susan K. Golant; *What to Do When Someone You Love is Depressed: A Practical, Compassionate, and Helpful Guide* (city, state: publisher, 2007), pp. 28, 31.

95 Michael E. Addis, Ph.D and Christopher R. Martell, Ph.D; *Overcoming Depression one Step at a Time: The New Behavioral Activation Approach to Getting Your Life Back* (city, state: publisher, 2004), pp. 38-43.

96 Armstrong and Best, *Courage After Fire*, p. 29.

97 Pam Rogers; email letter received September 14, 2012.

98 Diana Rahe Taylor; Toastmasters speech; September 26, 2012.

Chapter 13

99 *The New Encyclopedia of Christian Quotations*; Compiled by Mark Water; Baker Books; ©2000; Page 48

100 *Combat Trauma: A Personal Look at Long-Term Consequences*; Dr. James D. Johnson: © 2010; Page 88.

101 Ibid. Page 88.

102 *Once a Warrior Always a Warrior: Navigating the Transition from Combat to Home*; Charles W. Hoge, MD, Colonel, U.S. Army (Ret.); © 2010; Page 154.

103 *Combat Trauma: A Personal Look at Long-Term Consequences*; Dr. James D. Johnson; © 2010; Page 86.

104 Ibid.; Page 88.

105 Don Colbert, M.D.; *Deadly Emotions: Understand the Mind-Body-Spirit Connection that Can Heal or Destroy You*; Thomas Nelson Publishers; © 2003; Page 58.

106 James D. Johnson, PhD; *Combat Trauma: A Personal Look at Long-Term Consequences*; Rowman & Littlefield Publishers, Inc; © 2010; Page 59.

107 *Combat Trauma: A Personal Look at Long-Term Consequences;* James D. Johnson; Rowman & Littlefield Publishers, Inc.; © 2010; Pages 87-88.

108 W. Doyle Gentry, PhD; *Anger Management for Dummies*; Wiley Publishing, Inc.; © 2007; Page 22.

109 Ibid. Page 36.

110 Don Colbert, M.D.; *Deadly Emotions: Understand the Mind-Body-Spirit Connection that can Heal or Destroy you;* Thomas Nelson Publishers; © 2003; Page 50.

111 Ibid.

112 W. Doyle Gentry, PhD; *Anger Management for Dummies*; Wiley Publishing, Inc.; © 2007; Page 38.

113 W. Doyle Gentry, PhD; Anger Management for Dummies; Wiley Publishing, Inc.; © 2007; Page 61-63.

114 *Combat Trauma: A Personal Look at Long-Term Consequences;* James D. Johnson; Rowman & Littlefield Publishers, Inc.; © 2010; Pages 86-87.

115 Ibid. Page 139

116 John C. Maxwell; *Encouragement Changes Everything;* © 2008; Page 13.

117 Kennedy, John F., cited in David Zerfoss; *Stress is a Choice: 10 Rules to Simplify Your Life;* © 2011; Page 48.

118 David Zerfoss; *Stress is a Choice: 10 Rules to Simplify Your Life;* © 2011; Page 99; Quote by Mitch Albom.

119 Mac Anderson; Finding Joy: Simple Secrets to a Happy Life; Simple Truths Publishing; © 2008; Page 95.

120 Proverbs 17:22 NKJV

121 Allen Klein; *The Healing Power of Humor: Techniques for Getting through Loss, Setbacks, Upsets, Disappointments, Difficulties, Trials, Tribulations, and All That Not-So-Funny Stuff;* Jeremy P. Tarcher/Putnam a member of Penguin Putnam Inc.; ©1989; Page 18.

122 Don Colbert, M.D.; *Deadly Emotions: Understand the Mind-Body-Spirit Connection that Can Heal or Destroy You;* Thomas Nelson Publishers; ©2003; Page 35.

123 www.goodreads.com/author/quotes/8435.Norman_Vincent_Peale.

Chapter 14

124 Combat Trauma: A Personal Look at Long-Term Consequences; Dr. James D. Johnson; © 2010; Page 65.

125 Ibid. Page 68.

126 Mac Anderson; *One Choice: You're always One Choice Away From Changing Your Life;* Simple Truths © 2011; Page 22.

127 James Johnson, Ph.D.; *Combat Trauma: A Personal Look at Long-Term Consequences;* © 2010; Page 94

Chapter 15

128 Ibid; Page 93.

129 Ibid. Page 96.

130 *Miller-Keane Encyclopedia and Dictionary of Medicine, Nursing, and Allied Health;* Seventh Edition; © 2003.

131 Charles W. Hoge, MD, Colonel, U.S. Army (Ret.); *Once a Warrior Always a Warrior: Navigating the Transition from Combat to Home, Including Combat Stress, PTSD, and TBI;* Globe Pequot Press; Guilford, Connecticut; 2010; P 55.

132 Combat Trauma: A Personal Look at Long-Term Consequences; James D. Johnson; Rowman and Littlefield Publishers, Inc.; 2010; Page 79.

Chapter 16

133 Ibid; Page 135.

134 *Once a Warrior, Always a Warrior;* Charles W. Hoge, MD, U.S. Army (Ret.); GPP Life; Guilford, Connecticut; © 2010; Page 29

135 Ibid; Page 81.

136 Ibid; Page 96

137 Ibid; P. 96

138 Ibid; Page 96

139 Ibid.; Page 76

140 James. D. Johnson; *Combat Trauma: A Personal Look at Long-Term Consequences;* Rowman and Littlefield Publishers, Inc.; © 2010; Page 75-76.

141 Ibid; Page 77

142 Kendra Cherra; *What is Positive Thinking?;* About.com Psychology.

143 Dr. Lee Jampolsky; *Smile for No Good Reason: Simple Things You Can Do To Get Happy NOW.* Page 11.

144 Brent Agin, MD and Sharon Perkins, RN. *Healthy Aging for Dummies.* (New York: Wiley Publishing, Inc., 2008), p. _____.

Chapter 17

145 Ibid., p. 16.

146 Ibid., p. 188.

147 Ibid..

148 Ibid., p. 189.

149 Ibid., p. 274.

150 http://psychcentral.com/archives/2009/03/18/10-stress-busters/

151 Brent Agin, MD and Sharon Perkins, RN; Healthy Aging for Dummies; Wiley Publishing, Inc.; 2008; Pgs. 255-257

152 Shamash Alidina. *Mindfulness for Dummies* .(New York: John Wiley and Sons, Ltd, Publication, 2010), p. 12.

153 Mark Williams and Danny Penman; *An Eight-Week Plan for Finding Peace in a Frantic World;* Rodale; © 2011.

154 http://www.goodreads.com/author/quotes/23924.Martin_Luther_King_Jr_

155 John C. Maxwell. *Own Your Dreams: Discovering Your Purpose in Life.* (city, state: Simple Truths, LLC and Success Books, 2012), p. _____.

156 http://www.goodreads.com/author/quotes/223411.Golda_Meir

157 Ibid.

158 http://www.goodreads.com/quotes/tag/aging

159 James D. Johnson, *Combat Trauma: A Personal Look at Long-Term Consequences*; Rowman and Littlefield Publishers, Inc.; 2010; Page 55, 56.

160 Ibid; Page 62

161 Ibid; Page 62

162 http://www.macalester.edu/psychology/whathapp/ubnrp/nightmares/amightmares.htm.

163 Ibid.

164 http.//www.medicinenet.com/script/main/art.asp?articlekey=37618&pf=3&page=2

165 *In* Raymond Monsour Scurfield and Katherine Theresa Platoni; *Healing War Trauma: A Handbook of Creative Approaches; Ibid; 135*Routlegde Taylor and Francis Group, © 2013; Pages 133-135.

166 Ibid; Page 135.

167 Ibid; Page 135.

168 Ibid; Page 135.

169 http://www.medicinenet.com/script/main/art.asp?articlekey=37618&pf=3&page=2

170 James D. Johnson, *Combat Trauma: A Personal Look at Long-Term Consequences*; Rowman and Littlefield Publishers, Inc.; 2010; Page 62.

171 Ibid; Page 58.

172 Mark Goulston, MD; Post-Traumatic Stress Disorder for Dummies; Wiley Publishing, Inc.; © 2008; Page 231.

173 Ibid; Page 231.

174 Ibid; Page 231.

175 Sheldon G. Sheps, M.D.; Sleep Deprivation: A cause of high blood pressure; Mayo Clinic: http://www.mayoclinic.com/health/sleep-deprivation/AN01344.

176 Timothy Morgenthaler, M.D.; Lack of Sleep: Can it make you sick?; Mayo Clinic; http://www.mayoclinic.com/health/lack-of-sleep/An02065.

177 Ashley B. Hart II, Ph.D.; An Operators Manual for Combat PTSD: Essays for Coping; Writer's Showcase presented by Writer's Digest; © 2000; Page 146.

178 Ibid: Page 147.

179 Andy Andrews; *The Butterfly Effect: How Your Life Matters*; Simple Truths — Your Destination for Inspiration; www.simpletruths.com; © 2009.

180 Steven M. Southwick, MD and Dennis S. Charney, MD; Resilience: The Science of Mastering Life's Greatest Challenges; Cambridge University Press; © 2012; Pages 95-96.